FAITH
FAMILY
FINANCIAL
FREEDOM

A Young Couple's Gospel-Minded Journey out
of $230,000 of Student Loan Debt

AYANNA PATTERSON

Contents

Allow Us to Introduce Ourselves

We are the Pattersons - a young-*ish* couple who have been married since 2015. We have two children: an energetic boy and a bold girl, and we are so excited to share our family's financial journey with you! This book is intended to give you a peek into our struggles and triumphs as it relates to finances (especially our student loan debt) and married life with kids in hopes that we can help others who may feel set back or even crippled by their finances. As Christians, references to God and His word will frequent the pages of this book, as we believe He is our Provider and Waymaker, even when it seemed like we were at our "brokest" point. Our mission is to make it known that our dependence has been, is, and will continue to be on Him. We desire to point you to Him and remind you that faith and hope are found in the gospel for all seasons of life.

My husband and I met while we were in graduate school. We both received higher education with aspirations of attaining high-paying jobs after college. I graduated with my

Bachelor's and Master's in Chemical Engineering, and went on to work for a prestigious cosmetic company, making just over $50,000 right out of grad school. My husband graduated as a Doctor of Physical Therapy with a salary in the mid $60,000's. Bear in mind that these weren't exactly the salaries that those degrees promised when we first declared our majors. I remember saying to a mentor when I first entered the workforce, "I thought I'd start out earning more." Her response was, "Be patient. The money will come." Although we were both looking for a fat check, this advice towards patience and even contentment was an important lesson to learn early on in our careers. Proverbs 13:11 (ESV) says *"Wealth gained hastily will dwindle, but whoever gathers little by little will increase it."* I often wonder if getting too much too soon would have helped or hindered us on our financial journey. Would we have jumped to a B.M.F. (Blowing Money Fast) lifestyle, instead of learning to lead a life of consistent frugality to achieve our financial goals?

Before marriage, we received wise advice from our church's premarital counseling to discuss all of the taboo topics that many couples who are dating don't end up discussing until it turns into a huge fight later on in marriage: kids, finances, sex, family history, etc. As a part of these discussions we shared each other's salaries and credit scores, and we also revealed our debts to each other. It turned out that together, we were in pretty serious debt. No, no. You don't understand. Six-figure debt. We were over $230,000 neck-deep in student loan debt.

At times, it felt paralyzing, as though we were financially enslaved. We weren't always able to join our family and friends when they would ask us to go out to brunch or on a trip. We were mostly confined to the routine that consisted of leftovers and free (yet still romantic) escapes to the local park. Since we happen to share the same birthday, we made a date-day of making our rounds to any place that offered free birthday meals or treats! While we were often able to find a lot of joy in this cheap or free lifestyle, we didn't want to live in financial bondage forever. I know what you're thinking. '*You knew that y'all were going to be almost a quarter of a million dollars in debt, and still decided to go forward with marriage?*' YUP! We know that some couples choose to hit certain financial milestones such as getting their debt paid down before entering into marriage. But, we optimistically thought that surely a doctor and an engineer would be able to make it out of debt within just a few years. We did all the things we thought we were supposed to do: did our budget, saved, and set up our 401K retirement accounts.

Well, life happened and it happened fast. We experienced the financial speed bumps of having children and providing for their needs (including the exorbitant cost of childcare), becoming homeowners, paying for student loans and bills, and trying to save and invest, all while staying sane! We are going to keep it all the way real with you, being 100% transparent, by sharing our sacrifices, struggles, and frustrations.

Our goal is to leave a *legacy* that lasts for generations. Yes, we want to be debt-free. Yes, we want to have a significant net worth. Yes, we want our children to attend any college they want, debt-free. However, the legacy that we want to leave behind is not solely financial wealth. We want our children, and our children's children to understand the values of generosity, kindness, patience, and love; values that we believe come from intimately knowing the God who made heaven and earth, the God who gives and takes away. This is true wealth. Our goal in writing this book is laid out in 2 Corinthians 1:3-4: *"Blessed be the God and Father of our Lord Jesus Christ, the Father of mercies and God of all comfort, who comforts us in all our affliction, so that we may be able to comfort those who are in any affliction, with the comfort with which we ourselves are comforted by God."* We want our story, with all of our mistakes and discoveries to comfort you with gospel truths amid any financial affliction that you may be experiencing or may experience in the future. When it comes to hardship, financial, relational, or otherwise, you're either entering, exiting, or in the midst of it.

There are strategies, techniques, and tips that we've picked up along our journey that we will share with you. This book is not purely financial but also seeks to provide spiritual and relational advice that we consider to be our joyful obligation to share. These facets of life are interconnected. Spiritual disconnection can lead to money problems, which can then lead to relational problems. Fixing a financial issue at the surface level may still leave you feeling relationally broken.

I hope that if even one person is helped because of this book, then it has fulfilled its purpose. Each chapter will end with some key reflection questions that we hope will be helpful for you to think through individually or as a couple. You can feel free to write out answers in the space provided, in a journal, or just think or talk through them. These questions are meant to open your eyes to how God has made us different and placed us in unique situations, which have shaped us to be the ever-changing people that we are today. They will also give insight into why we are the way that we are when it comes to money. Why are some people natural-born spenders, while others hold tightly to their money? Why do some people use coupons, while others don't even glance at prices? Is it possible to shift your mindset after you've spent your entire life being shaped into who you are today? Due to these differences, finances can be a major point of contention in a relationship. Understanding one another and being prayerful together will help strengthen your relationship. This, of course, is a general statement, but we've found that it is especially true in the area of finances. Please join us on our journey to loving the Lord, losing the loans, and gaining both financial and spiritual freedom, while growing closer together!

Financial Heritage

A person's financial heritage is the familial and historical narrative, which has a direct or indirect impact on the way that person handles, thinks, and feels about money. Some families pass down their financial knowledge from generation to generation, while others keep it locked away because of ignorance of its importance or even shame of its mishandling. In the same way that it's important to know and understand history because it can repeat itself, it's also important to know and understand financial heritage. Many Black people in America have painful financial roots that trace back to when they were sold and treated as property. This free labor laid the financial foundation of this country from which whites primarily benefited and continue to benefit. "Slavery, 'America's original sin,' according to James Madison, created the foundation of modern American capitalism. It was slavery and the "blood drawn with the lash" that opened the arteries of capital and commerce that led to U.S. economic dominance worldwide. The effects of the institution of slavery on American commerce were monumental—3.2 million slaves were worth $1.3 billion in market value, almost equal to the entire gross national product." [1]

Slavery and the racism that accompanied it play a major part in the financial heritage in the present lives of many Black people today. Whether it's being red-lined into the ghettos of a city or being paid a fraction of the salary obtained by whites, racism continues to haunt the financial come-up of Black people. It is commonly discussed in Black communities that whites know how to play the so-called money game, and that they pass this secret knowledge down through the generations. This idea has motivated many Black people, myself included, to learn this game and educate others on how to close this racial wealth gap while remaining cognizant of the written and unwritten rules designed for whites to win and Blacks to lose. "The wealth gap is where the injustices sown in the past grow imperceptibly in the present. The cumulative effects of discrimination, segregation, and the economic detour for black businesses have created self-perpetuating forces that continue to make black wealth accumulation difficult." [2]

"Today, black families have an average net wealth of $11,000 compared to a white family's average of $141,900. Pew data

---

[1] Mehrsa Baradaran, *The Color of Money: Black Banks and the Racial Wealth Gap, 10*

[2] Ibid, 249

reveals that white families have thirteen times more wealth than black families. The wealth gap exists at every income and education level. On average, white families with college degrees have over $300,000 more wealth than black families with college degrees. A third of black families have no assets at all. Moreover, studies reveal that the gap is accelerating—over the last thirty years, the average wealth of white families has grown at three times the rate for average black families. This growing divide perpetuates injustices hard to capture behind the latest news of riots and protests." [3]

I would be remiss if I didn't explain that the financial heritage of America as a whole and the direct and indirect consequences that it has on Black people, my people, is a personal driver for why I'm writing this book. I hope that this book cultivates increased awareness of this problem and that people would be inspired to seek education and take personal action to mitigate the effects of financial bondage.

In my family, we have relatives who we consider to be the family genealogists, who can trace our family back to slavery and beyond, and there are lots of stories that have been passed down. I am blessed to have a family that openly discusses success, failure, and trauma, whether financial or otherwise. We seek to learn and grow from it, all in hopes of doing better than the previous generations. We love and

---

[3] Ibid, 249

support one another's aspirations, and yield to one another's wisdom and experiences.

I start the story of my financial heritage with my grandmother and grandfather, affectionately known as Mom-Mom and Pop-Pop. They both grew up as Black folks in the foothills of the Blue Ridge mountains in North Carolina. They were considered poor by many people's standards, yet never lacked joy. Like many Black people in that era, they made their way up to a Northern city as part of the Great Migration to earn better wages and escape the overt racism of the South. "The Great Migration, which lasted roughly from 1910 until 1970, radically transformed the country. During this seismic shift, approximately six million blacks left the south. In 1900, ninety percent of black Americans lived in the rural areas of Southern states. By 1970, 80 percent of black Americans lived in urban areas and nearly half outside the South. Blacks left the South because of racial injustice and the general decline of economic conditions below the Mason-Dixon line. They were pulled to the North by the promise of better jobs, better pay, and more opportunities for advancement." [4] Pop-Pop found work in a factory in New Jersey and was an exceptional carpenter both by hobby and vocation. Almost all the cabinets, wooden furniture, and even some toys at Mom-Mom and Pop-Pop's

---

[4] Ibid, 69

house were made by his skillful hands. Mom-Mom migrated up North when my mom was just six months old, experiencing the weight of the Jim Crow South lifted from her as she moved to the front of the bus for the first time after crossing over the Mason-Dixon line. She worked cleaning houses of wealthy white people for only a few dollars a day and told stories of scrubbing the floors on her hands and knees. Because Pop-Pop served in World War II, they were qualified to live in housing designed for war veterans and their families, which is now known as "the projects." During this time, Mom-Mom earned her real estate sales and broker's licenses and was instrumental in facilitating home ownership for her own family, as well as many other African American families. If she sold a home to an African American family, residents who did not want to live in proximity to Blacks would move, known as "white flight." As more white residents moved, the result was more homes for sale in better neighborhoods. This allowed the listing and sales of more homes. This effort opened the doors to home ownership for African Americans in neighborhoods not previously opened to them. Mom-Mom later went on to earn both her Bachelor's and Master's degrees and soared in her career with the city government becoming an expert in city planning, architecture, and the historical integrity of housing and property. [5] Both Mom-Mom and Pop-Pop worked to ensure that their children and all their descendants could live better lives than they lived. Mom-Mom daily spoke of the brightness that she saw in each of her children, grandchildren, and great-grandchildren, telling us that we were "just like the lightning bug; we got the 'stuff' in us."

To further elaborate on my financial heritage, my mom gave birth to me much later in life, in her forties. Although she was a single parent, she had become financially established in life. By the time she had me, she had already received her Bachelor's and Master's degrees. She finished her dissertation for her Doctorate with me wrapped tightly to her as a baby. She was able to leverage some financial aid to give me private school education from grades 6-12 after the public school system began to hinder my learning pace. I tagged along with her as her travel sidekick on trips to the Bahamas, Puerto Rico, and even a trip to France for a family wedding (gifted to us by Pop-Pop). I was also blessed to be able to go on trips with my schools to Guatemala, Nicaragua, and China, which allowed me to obtain a global perspective.

As a child, I would often spend the night at Mom-Mom and Pop-Pop's house, while she attended late-night meetings,

---

[5] Adapted from *Hidden Figure - Rebecca Rousseau Mitchell: Neighborhood Planner, Bureau Chief, God's Special Child*

positioning herself to one day be Vice President at a community college. She became well-known in the community for being a servant leader. She is the kind of woman who once bought a coat for one of her students who said they couldn't make it to class because it was Winter, and they didn't have the funds to purchase one of their own. Countless times, when the financial aid wasn't enough to cover books, she reached into her own pockets to ensure "her kids" didn't have any roadblocks to an education. She tirelessly fought systemic injustice within academia and spoke up for the voiceless. I also watched her write a check every Sunday during church to tithe and donate to organizations that she was passionate about. I learned what generosity looked like by watching her selflessly give to others.

She also taught me about saving and investing. As a teenager, she would show me the mutual fund statements that she had set up in my name. I remember tuning out, as words like "dividends," "interest," and "return on investment" went over my head. At the time, my teenage brain was busy thinking about boys or going to the mall with friends instead. We led a life, not so much of frugality, but convenience. My mom was already well into her fifties by then, busy with work, and simply didn't have time or energy to "DIY" anything. Mowing lawns, plowing snow, painting walls, and cleaning the house were all things that she just paid someone to do. This was my normal; some might say I was a little spoiled or bougie. Imagine my surprise when I discovered that the rest of the world, including my future husband, didn't grow up like this.

The memory of my husband's financial heritage begins very similarly to mine. His great-grandparents were also a part of the Great Migration of Blacks from the South to New York City. Both his great-grandparents and grandparents lived in the projects for most of their lives as well. His parent's generation was the first to "make it out" and achieve home ownership. His dad, a bus driver for the MTA, was always out of the house for work before sunrise and came home exhausted from a long day of driving. He was the frugal one in their relationship, while his mom, who worked in finance, was in charge of handling money for the family, but was more of a spender. Her drive and motivation to do better for herself and her family led to her purchasing their first home at the age of twenty-five when my husband was eight years old. She even used the money stashed in my husband's piggy bank toward the down payment for the house, a step closer to financial freedom, although an eight-year-old may not have understood the importance at the time. Opposite to my upbringing, they were very much a "DIY" family. Mowing the lawn, shoveling snow, and fixing what was broken were family activities that brought them together, even if it was to my husband's dismay. Both the motivation of his mom and the frugality of his dad were passed down to my husband, as he began to learn to navigate through finances in his own life. He watched his mom clip coupons and accompanied his dad to Canal street to buy knockoff items at a reduced price. He even had a side-hustle while working at a fast-food restaurant in high school, where he would sell peel-off stickers with a winning prize of a free meal to his friends. He was known both in high school and college to never buy food or drinks when out with friends and was nicknamed "the cheap one". While he may have been mocked for living frugally, the lessons learned from his financial heritage dwelled with him through adulthood and made him a very wise spender.

Our financial heritages of the past have shaped how we view money in the present. When two financial heritages that are starkly different come together in a relationship, there can be some friction. It certainly caused conflict in our marriage. It's important to give space for these differences in financial heritage when in a committed relationship. It's important to note and be sensitive that some people may have a financial heritage with trauma attached. Some may have experienced or witnessed relationships where money was used as a manipulative or abusive tool. Perhaps there were times of lack that caused someone to stay in survivor's mode, holding tightly onto money, even if in reality there was plenty of money in the bank. Whether your financial heritage is one of trauma or treasure, give grace and space, without judgment to your partner. Knowing your financial heritage lays the groundwork for you to be able to communicate and gradually adapt your mindset to faithfully plan for your financial future.

Reflection Questions

1. Have you and your spouse discussed your financial heritage?
2. How far back can you trace your financial heritage?
3. What is the money story of your parents and grandparents?
4. How has their money story shaped your own?
5. In what ways are you and your spouse's money stories different or the same?
6. Have the effects of your financial heritage caused conflict?
7. What financial traumas or treasures have you experienced or witnessed?

Two Become One

Our family heritages molded us into two very different people in lots of different areas of our lives, but our worlds uncomfortably collided when it came to managing finances together. My husband is the frugal one, and I tend to be more of a spender. This is evidence of the money mindsets that have developed from over 30 years of our experiences, from what we've been taught, and from our own independent personalities. Even though these differences were lightly discussed before marriage, we had a very difficult transition after we jumped the broom. There was a chasm of inexperience between talking about our differences and then actually living these differences out. We decided before marriage, with wise counsel from our spiritual mentors, to merge our bank accounts. Many couples may choose to do this differently, and that's okay. This is what works for us based on our belief that this builds trust and transparency in marriage. There are no secrets, and we are both able to have full visibility of our combined finances. There is no *mine* versus *his* anymore; it's all *ours* (with one small caveat of an allowance).

Due to my previously mentioned family background, I had an Arianna Grande "I want it, I got it" outlook on life. Before marriage, getting my nails done every two weeks, and purchasing $200 boots or a plane ticket with money I saved, was normal behavior. I lived at home with my mom for two years after getting a job, so my bills were few and I enjoyed the occasional splurge. Treating myself was encouraged since I had always been a hard worker with ambition. Looking at price tags for groceries or buying generic products instead of brand-name products were foreign concepts to me. Don't misunderstand; I was not unwise with my money. In fact, I was able to gleefully splurge and still sock away $10,000, all while putting extra money toward my student loans. Due to my "Type A" personality, I naturally set up spreadsheets and diligently did my budget each month to determine what I could afford. Allocating my funds and setting aside reward money was fun for me. I had a credit card that was set up as a joint account with my mom while I was in college, but I only used it for textbooks and emergencies, such as an unexpected car repair, and always paid it off as quickly as possible. I ran all credit card purchases by my mom first and never used it for retail therapy. She had made me aware of interest rates higher than 20%, and the impact that could have on my pockets, so I stayed far away from consumer debt. Using my credit card in this way was enough to have a good starting point to build a healthy credit score.

My husband lived a bit of a different lifestyle when I met him. Truly in broke college student mode, he ate cereal for dinner most nights to save money. I enjoyed cooking up a meal and bringing it to the study center while he buried his head in his books. The saying "The way to a man's heart is his stomach" certainly rang true for my man. His work-study job at the university's gym helped him pay for rent and utilities. He lived a very frugal lifestyle (dare I say cheap). To his roommates' dismay, he wrote a note, disallowing them to turn on the thermostat above 69 degrees in the middle of Winter. He jokingly mandated that everyone better layer up! Needless to say, I didn't spend a lot of time in his apartment in the Winter, and this is not a mandate that goes over well in the Patterson household today!

Bumpin' Heads

Reality hit both of us when we got back from the honeymoon and settled into real married life. Now is a good time to mention that we did not live together before marriage. There was no real "practice" at doing life together, which in hindsight, I still wouldn't change. My husband was baffled at how I could ever spend $3 on Oreos when I could have waited a day for the 2 for $5 sale. Sales just weren't something that had caught my attention. I never grabbed the flyer positioned at the front of the store for review. I had never even clipped a coupon. At first, I couldn't believe that he was being serious. My disbelief quickly turned to anxiety because

I felt like I was not *allowed* to get something that I wanted just because it cost an extra 50 cents. He repeatedly explained to me how an extra 50 cents adds up over the course of a large shopping trip. While I understood that concept, I didn't have the years of experience to decipher between a good sale and a bad one. I grocery shopped with my mom all the time, and never once saw her use a coupon and never got told to put something back on the shelf due to its cost. The only restriction that I remember her setting for herself was to never buy orange juice if it cost more than three dollars, from which she taught me about supply and demand. She would say, *"If collectively, we don't buy it, the price will drop soon."*

It wasn't just groceries. I had begun working out and started experiencing some foot pain and realized I needed new sneakers since mine were several years old. This wasn't some impulsive purchase I wanted to make, but I did want a high-quality shoe that would last me a few years. My philosophy with shoes (especially leather boots) is to spend the extra money on high-quality shoes instead of having to buy cheap shoes every year that wear out quickly. Well, hubby was on board with the purchase but assured me that the sneakers I wanted could be found at a better price if I waited for a sale or found a coupon. This type of back-and-forth created quite a bit of tension between us early in our marriage. We needed to figure out a way to compromise. As believers united together in Christ, we knew that part of marriage was living sacrificially and dying to our own selfish desires. It was time for both of us to put this into practice.

At the advice of our spiritual mentors, we chose to allot an equal amount of spending money to each of us that we would designate as an allowance. While doing our budget for the month, we reviewed our expected income and expenses, then decided on the amount together. There were times when we had to forgo allowance altogether due to budgeting constraints, and there were also times when we could each get a little extra (usually around Christmas time). The amount varied per month and would go into a separate checking account to which the other did not have visibility. This gave my husband, the frugal one, the ability to save. Out of his love and generosity, he'd save enough to buy me a present. And this gave me, the splurger, the ability to spend $14 on chocolate or Dunkin' Donuts® with only a little bit of judgment from him. (Side note: To this day, 90% of my allowance continues to go to food or coffee!) Occasionally, I would also save to buy hubby a little something that I thought would bring him joy. Receiving an allowance was particularly important to me because it gave me a piece of freedom that, truth be told, I felt I had lost when getting married to a frugal person.

Grace and Mercy

Two becoming one is also about having a gracious and merciful mindset regarding what debt or credit scores are brought into the marriage. Neither of us had consumer debt from credit cards, however, my husband brought with him the bulk of the student loan debt. Many men understand that the weight of being a husband includes being a provider, and some men have insecurities about not being able to provide in the way that they would like. It was important in our relationship for him to know that I didn't think of him or his debt as a burden to me in any way. His debt was now *our* debt, and we would tackle it together, and rejoice over each dollar that we paid back to the lender: TOGETHER. My job as a wife is to encourage and uplift, and to repent in areas where I may have made him feel insecure about the debt he brought to the marriage or his ability to provide. His character (patient, kind, thoughtful, funny, and while not a part of his character, I'll add fine) was worth much more than this financial setback. I was well aware of his ambition and work ethic and knew that we would be just fine. Also, I had full trust that the Lord would help us to overcome this hurdle.

Leaving and Cleaving

One part of two becoming one that was difficult for me was the idea of leaving and cleaving. Genesis 2:24 (ESV) says,

"Therefore a man shall leave his father and his mother and hold fast to his wife, and they shall become one flesh." Traditionally, this meant from a financial perspective that the woman's father was no longer her provider, but that now her husband would take care of all her needs. There was still a part of me that nostalgically longed for the convenience of my childhood. "Can't you just pay someone to do it?" still occasionally comes out of my mouth. And there were many times when I tried to propose asking for my mom's financial assistance. This was not a helpful dynamic in a relationship where my husband desired to be the provider for our family. It was much more a matter of principle than practice. He felt as though asking for help was like taking a handout for something that he desired to work hard for. He was okay with the wait and was not in any rush to have it *right now*. This gave him a sense of purpose in his headship over our family. I needed to learn to leave the comforts of my mom and her assistance, and cleave first to God and secondly to my husband. With this, I also needed to learn patience with not getting what I wanted right away. There is a joy that comes with delayed gratification. We are currently living in a world where the thing you want can be delivered to your doorstep on the same day that your purchased it. I grew up listening to the AOL dial tone sometimes for more than ten minutes just to get connected to the internet (showing my age here). Online shopping, where I could order same-day delivery was once not - a - thing. There was a time when

everything wasn't so instant. Just because we now live in an instantaneous society, does not mean that patience no longer has a place in our lives. To eliminate debt and reach financial freedom, patience and self-control (Fruit of the Spirit alert!) are of the utmost importance. So over time, I learned that it was okay to say no thank you to my mom, who I knew was willing to come to our rescue. It felt almost like a rites of passage into adulthood to become more dependent on God than on her.

The Merge

Two becoming one meant that as we spent more time together, we were more willing to humble ourselves, concede to, and even adopt the other's viewpoint. For me, it meant that clipping coupons (paper and digital) and reviewing the store flyers became a normal pre-shopping ritual. It meant that I wouldn't always be able to get my beloved Oreos if they weren't on sale. When shopping together, my husband and I would watch the eye rolls and attitude of the cashier as we handed them our dozens of coupons and tried to guess how much our groceries would ring up to. Watching the total cost fall dramatically after all coupons had been scanned became a fun game for us. I'm now experiencing moments of frugality, where I thought to myself, I *never* would have done this five years ago!

For instance, I was recently doing a Walmart run and noticed that Halloween candy was on sale, 90% off. The chocolate lover in me rejoiced and I made the purchase! I got to my car and checked the receipt to find out that they had only given me 75% off. Now in my pre-marital days, I would have shrugged and popped open that bag on my drive home (or not even noticed the switcheroo in the first place because I never reviewed receipts). But now that two had become one, and we had achieved "the merge" in our marriage, I found myself getting out of my car to stand in a customer service line for 20 minutes to get $2.20 back into our bank account. What a transformation! When I told my husband the story of my heroic cheapness, he got down on one knee and re-proposed to me. Many of you may be thinking, "That's a little extreme," but there is a mindset shift that occurs when trying to make a true financial change that will benefit your pockets in the long run.

For my husband, two becoming one meant that it was okay to save and splurge on a fancy date night or purchase a nice pair of shoes for himself. We became the checks and balances for each other in the life we were building together. Our shared goals, such as becoming debt-free, investing for our retirement, and saving for our children's education became our motivation to set our sights on wise financial stewardship. This is not to say that we don't still bump heads on financial decisions, but for us, there was a clear transition into financial intimacy, where trust, humility, and oneness flowed between us. As one who desires to see successful marriages, especially in the Church, it is my hope that this merge and intimacy of all types can be achieved and maintained.

Reflection Questions

1. Who is the frugal one and who is the splurger in your relationship?
2. What financial challenges have you faced while becoming one?
3. Do you have a plan for your family's finances: combined or separate accounts? Allowance or free-spending?
4. Do you have mentors who can guide you through challenges?
5. How do you view the debt or credit scores that each has brought into the marriage? Is there grace and mercy that you need to extend?
6. Are there areas where you need to leave and cleave?

God Loves a Cheerful Giver

One mindset that we teach our children, but have a hard time grasping ourselves, is that nothing on this earth truly belongs to us. In the same way a landlord is the actual owner of a house, and the tenants just occupy space there and pay rent, that is also how we are all just temporary tenants in this earthly home. We are to live life here respecting our temporary possessions and giving thanks to God as the true owner of it all. When my 5-year-old son (at the time of writing this), yells "MINE!" as he tug-of-wars a car with his little sister, I say, "Nothing is yours. It all belongs to God." This is an effort to reframe his selfish mindset to one that is more capable of sharing. James 1:17 (ESV) says *"Every good and every perfect gift is from above, coming down from the Father of lights, with whom there is no variation or shadow due to change."* While we are here on this earth, our job is to simply steward our money, possessions, and time in a way that brings God glory. I'd like to add that we will consistently fail at doing this. A part of us, even as adults, will go into "MINE!" mode, forgetting that a part of our purpose on earth is to show love, kindness, and generosity. A part of us desires to selfishly live life with a clenched fist, not willing to let go of our worldly possessions.

Why would a couple who is $230,000 in student loan debt choose to allocate their extra money to any place other than their student loans? For us, the answer is simple: God is sovereign over every penny that comes into and goes out of our lives. He is our Provider and has shown Himself to be faithful time and time again. As good stewards over what He has blessed us with, we choose to give Him a portion of our income, which ultimately belongs to Him anyway. When people think of the word worship, they may think of singing with eyes tightly shut and hands lifted, dancing, or prayer. All true, but tithing is another way we can honor and worship God. Every Sunday at church, we answer the following questions with scripture in a call-and-response style:

Who is the owner of all things?

For the Lord is a great God and a great King above all gods. In His hand are the depths of the earth; the heights of the mountains are His also. The sea is His, for He made it, and His hands formed the dry land.

Psalms 95:3-5 (ESV)

Who provides for us?

Oh come, let us worship and bow down; let us kneel before the Lord, our Maker! For He is our God, and we are the people of His pasture, and the sheep of His hand.

Psalms 95:6-7a (ESV)

How are we to respond?

Oh come, let us sing to the Lord; let us make a joyful noise to the rock of our salvation! Let us come into His presence with thanksgiving; let us make a joyful noise to Him with songs of praise!

Psalms 95:1-2 (ESV)

How should we give?

The point is this: whoever sows sparingly will also reap sparingly, and whoever sows bountifully will also reap bountifully. Each one must give as he has decided in his heart, not reluctantly or under compulsion, for God loves a cheerful giver.

2 Corinthians 9:6-7 (ESV)

I love reciting these verses every week because it resets how I think and feel about our money and our belongings. It's quite easy to become either prideful, thinking I have what I have because I work hard and I'm getting what I deserve; or become nonchalant by becoming accustomed to living a first-world life without giving thanks to the One who provided it all. It's also easy to become discontent, feeling as though you don't have enough and life would be better off with more. It truly takes a weekly reminder to recall who owns (God), who provides (God), how I should respond (praise, worship, thanksgiving, rejoicing), and what action I should take (give).

This mindset is not necessarily an easy one to come by for multiple reasons. Not all churches or organizations utilize the funds that they receive with integrity. My husband once attended a church in Philadelphia full of people living in poverty, who were manipulated into giving their money to a pastor who flaunted his expensive suits, gator shoes, and fancy cars, while his congregation sat in need. These types of pastors exist on television and all over the world, and they do a disservice to the churches that are honest with their money. They also do a disservice to potential church-goers who rightfully are unable to trust the church overall because of this dishonesty and financial abuse. My prayer is that this broken trust be rebuilt by churches and pastors that have financial integrity and who care about God's kingdom agenda more than personal profit.

Additionally, I am saddened at the proclamation of the so-called "prosperity gospel." This type of preaching falsely promises that giving more money to the church will result in supernatural healing and material blessings and that a life of suffering is not intended for Christians. 1 Peter 5:10 is quite clear that "*after you have suffered a little while, the God of all grace, who has called you to his eternal glory in Christ, will himself restore, confirm, strengthen, and establish you.*" The prosperity gospel forces a materialistic view of the biblical principle of reaping what you sow. The following verses all contain this principle:

"*Whoever sows injustice will reap calamity, and the rod of his fury will fail.*" <u>*Proverbs 22:8*</u> *(ESV)*

"*The wicked earns deceptive wages, but one who sows righteousness gets a sure reward.*" *Proverbs 11:18 (ESV)*

"*Those who sow in tears shall reap with shouts of joy!*" *Psalm 126:5 (ESV)*

"*Do not be deceived: God is not mocked, for whatever one sows, that will he also reap. For the one who sows to his own flesh will from the flesh reap corruption, but the one who sows to the Spirit will from the Spirit reap eternal life.*" *Galatians 6:7-8 (ESV)*

In these verses, things that can be sown include injustice, righteousness, tears, and sowing to the flesh or to the Spirit. Things that can be reaped include calamity, a sure reward, joy, corruption, and eternal life. Sowing and reaping means that our actions, whether positive or negative, godly or ungodly, have consequences. It refers to the condition of the heart, holy or evil. It does not connect the giving of money to our own financial or health-related come-up. Our desire should be to reap the sanctification of our hearts and to look more and more like Christ.

The prosperity gospel claims that if you just have enough faith, you can speak your desires for material wealth into existence or a terminal illness out of existence; if you don't receive your desired outcome, it's because your faith was too small. God is a God who deeply cares for us, who can perform miracles, and do the impossible. However, His heart is not to link His power to getting more money into the pockets of a greedy false teacher. God graciously still acts when we have small faith. Metaphorically, it just needs to be the size of a mustard seed, only a millimeter in diameter, to move mountains (see Matthew 17:20). Remember, God does not *need* our money; He is self-sufficient without receiving anything from us. Part of giving is about moving forward the kingdom of God on earth. The other part is about keeping a heart that is submissive to God and humble enough to see money as not truly belonging to us.

We are blessed that we completely trust the pastors and elders at our church who care for our spirits by preaching the true gospel and who transparently share how the money is being used. We are reminded of God's provision and faithfulness to us throughout the years. We are blown away by how God uses what we and the other members give to our local church to positively impact the surrounding community. We are a witness to how our church consistently meets both the spiritual and physical needs, through both local and global missions. It excites us to hear about our church's future plans to provide education and help build up businesses in the area.

I'm also reminded of my mom's consistent generosity, faithfully tithing each Sunday and donating wherever she saw a need. On so many occasions, we have been the recipients of God's grace. Like the old church would say, "We have a roof over our heads, clothes on our backs, and stomachs that have never gone hungry!" It's only right to cheerfully, not begrudgingly, give back to God what rightfully belongs to Him in the first place.

We recognize that God is the true owner of all things, that our response should be one of thanksgiving, and that because we are thankful, we should cheerfully give. While this concept might be simple, it's not always an easy mindset to have. We told you we were going to keep it real, so here's the truth. There have been times when we looked at our budget and silently thought to ourselves, "We could pay off our loans x number of years sooner if we just tithed a little less." Or "We could go on a nice little rendezvous to a tropical island if we just skipped a month or two of tithing."

There are lots of ways our deceitful hearts try to justify reasons to give less or not at all. We've been tempted toward selfish stewardship of our resources, which might make us feel good, but only momentarily. We want the lasting joy that comes from giving generously. Similarly, selfish is the heart that only gives with the expectation of receiving something in return. We don't give to get. We should never have a greedy mindset that believes God owes us *anything*. If the Lord chooses to provide more of something after we give, that is His grace alone; and it's our duty to gratefully and humbly accept with thankful hearts.

Each month, my husband and I sit down to do our budget and allocate our money to the various necessities of life. Matthew 6:21 (ESV) says *"For where your treasure is, there your heart will be also."* We do our best to give God our "firstfruits" to demonstrate to Him where our hearts truly lie. We feel as though it isn't most honoring to God to receive a paycheck, and then spend it on shopping or even bills, without even giving Him the thanks He deserves through tithing. It's pretty easy to tell where a person's heart is by looking at how they allocate their money and when.

Each month (to this very day), our expenses somehow exceed our income by hundreds, sometimes thousands of dollars! There have been many times when there was more month than money; when we had to revert to a cereal-for-dinner lifestyle. During these times, our mortgage, bills, and student loans still somehow got paid, and we were able to feed our family. It just doesn't make logical sense! In times like that, all we can do is shake our heads in bewilderment, and give thanks to the awesome God we serve, who chooses to ensure that we have always had everything we need to not only survive but also thrive!

Ultimately, God exemplifies generosity not only by the grace and mercy that He shows us each day but by giving His only Son, Jesus. There is no greater form of generosity. In a plan set before the foundations of the earth were laid, He anticipated that His people would fall and require a Savior. He sent Christ to this earth as a baby, who grew up to teach us how to live and love. Christ's best lesson on love was willingly trusting His Father and going to the cross. He laid down His life for our sins so that everyone who puts their trust in Him gains access to the Father and eternal life. John 15:13 (ESV) says *"Greater love has no one than this, that someone lay down his life for his friends."* God shows the greatest love and generosity by sacrificing His life to become the atonement that we desperately need. How can we not take the time and the effort to give back to Him, in tithe, in praise, in complete worship?

Reflection Questions

1. How do you feel about tithing? Are you and your partner on the same page?
2. Have you had any experiences that encouraged or discouraged you from tithing?
3. What are your thoughts about God's provision in your life?
4. Do you have an opened or closed hand when it comes to generosity?

The Budget

Before jumping into the importance and the how-to's of budgeting, there is a self-assessment that must take place before moving forward. Often, before making the decision to budget, there is a general unawareness of the motives that drive spending. Most people tend to make subconscious decisions when spending money. Getting to the emotional or mental roots can prove to be very helpful for curbing bad spending habits. I'm very self-aware that I choose to spend my allowance on coffee, chocolate, and other types of delicious foods, which I consider to be my business and mine alone. Most of those purchases are not planned, but are impulsive, driven by basic marketing and advertising. Just seeing a company's logo on a billboard can cause me to take the next exit so that I can experience the deliciousness of whatever drive-thru beckons me. Additionally, my purchases can be driven by a mood: I had such a long, crazy day. I deserve (pride-alert) this caramel frappaccino.

There are lots of motivations that cause us to spend money; sometimes out of necessity such as grocery shopping, but other times out of craving. I, myself, am no longer much of a clothes or shoes shopper, but some people love to swipe their cards at the mall or while watching QVC. They see something that appeals to their eye and experiences a "gotta have it" emotion. Referred to as retail therapy, sometimes negative events in our lives can cause us to cope by spending money on things that we think will make us feel happier. Often, this happiness is only temporary. So when we look at our budgets, and we review how our money has been spent over the past months, check-in with yourself mentally and emotionally on some of those "gotta have it" purchases. It's a no-judgment zone here (says the chocoholic), so I'm not necessarily making a recommendation to stop these purchases, but it's the moments of self-awareness that can allow you to decide what future decisions you make with your money.

Budgeting is a crucial part of having healthy finances because it's impossible to grow if you are consistently taking steps backward. Even if they are just tiny steps, they are cumulative. Living within your means, and even better, living well below your means is the chief idea behind financial stability. Most people know how much their paycheck is. Payday is a day to rejoice! It's evidence of the hard work that you've put in throughout the previous weeks. In an unfulfilling job, it might be the only thing motivating you to get up and go to work at all. It would be a shame to work so hard and then realize that for reasons within your control, you are spending more money than you're making. I also realize that for some, us included for a time, spending more than you're making may be completely out of your control. In those situations, doing everything you can to cut spending and increase income is what becomes key. This could mean searching for a higher paying job, setting up a side hustle, or selling some things.

Many people see budgeting as a hassle, a time consumer, and overall, not worth it. I would wholeheartedly disagree. A quote by architect Frank Lloyd Wright says, "You can use an eraser on the drafting table or a sledgehammer on the construction site." [6] While this may be a reference to architecture, the same sentiment applies to budgeting. It's an amazing opportunity to be able to do some planning to build something beautiful over the long run. I would think that physically taking a sledgehammer to the construction site might be devastating and costly for an architect who improperly measured or miscalculated. But when I think of how that analogy translates to one's finances, the effects of improper planning could be detrimental. Scripture affirms that *"The plans of the diligent lead surely to abundance, but everyone who is hasty comes only to poverty."* Proverbs 21:5 (ESV)

---

[6] Frank Lloyd Wright quote

Except for large purchases like the mortgage or daycare, our spending throughout the month is a bunch of small decisions. On average, we perform over sixty financial transactions per month. In the moment, five dollars here or 20 dollars there doesn't seem like that much. It's not until you do a comprehensive review of spending for the whole month that you fully realize the amount of money spent as well as the spending categories. It's this overarching view that enables you to recognize trends and the possible need for change. Realizing just how often you've fallen victim to the allure of Target's temptations may increase your desire to save, invest, or donate that amount spent on Target in the following month.

Another important point to make is that budgeting is very personal and unique to our family and our spending habits. We believe that it gives us the best view of our income and where our money is going. However, there may be a different way to do it that works better for your family, and that's great! But start somewhere and modify until you have something that works for you. Perhaps Excel spreadsheets are your thing. Or maybe you'd prefer an app to do all the work. Maybe you're old-school and pencil and paper are your jam. No judgment! There is no actual right way to budget. Lots of people will claim that they've unlocked that perfect budgeting method and convince you to do it their way. My recommendation is to survey lots of methods and determine which combination of those methods works best.

I already mentioned that I was a spreadsheet junkie. As an engineer, I love math and numbers and formulas, so much so, that I tortured myself by taking Calc 5 in college. So I was ready to put my expertise to the test in marriage with this budgeting stuff! Before marriage, I got over my distrust of technology and started using a budgeting app linked to my bank accounts. The app allows you to visualize how much money is flowing in and out. It also categorizes what you are spending your money on and alerts you if you've gone over budget in a particular category so that better choices can be made in the future. There are all types of ways to track and trend. For example, you can see how much money has been going toward food each month for the past six months. You can also review saving habits over the past year or see how your income has increased since entering the workforce. There are pie charts and bar graphs that make this math nerd's heart sing!

So, we combined incomes and bank accounts and continued to use this app in marriage. Each month, near the first and last of the month, we sit down together, begin our budgeting time in prayer. We always acknowledge and thank our God for how He has blessed and provided for us, as well as ask Him to guide us on how to wisely allocate our money in a way that is glorifying to Him. Since financial strife is a leading cause of divorce and our financial upbringings were starkly different, we knew that the enemy could and would attempt to use money to drive a wedge between us. We utilize prayer as a hedge of protection from the enemy's schemes during budget time. Even still, there were times when small disagreements could erupt into arguments over how money should be stewarded or how it got spent in the previous month. It's important to stay alert to how sneaky the enemy is and be cognizant of his attacks. *"Be sober-minded; be watchful. Your adversary the devil prowls around like a roaring lion, seeking someone to devour. Resist him, firm in your faith, knowing that the same kinds of suffering are being experienced by your brotherhood throughout the world."* 1 Peter 5:8-9 (ESV) Remember that he hates marriage, and enjoys any bickering that may happen during budget time. Stay prayed up, and know that your spouse is not your enemy. Live life in light of eternity, knowing that budgeting does not even exist in heaven! Isaiah 40:7 (ESV) says *"The grass withers, the flower fades,"* and I add, so do budgets. While budgeting has an important impact here on earth, it's still just temporary.

We found a template of a budgeting spreadsheet on the internet and adjusted it to match the categories we had chosen in the budgeting app that we use: Income, Savings, Charity/Gifts, Student Loans, Home (which included mortgage, water, sewer, electric, and home warranty), Auto, Food, Shopping (cough cough Target and Walmart), Health, Kids, Personal Care, Allowances, and the Credit Card. Even as I write this, I pretty much know the categories by heart.

We meet at the beginning of the month to tell our money where it should go. Then, we meet near the end of the month to see how we did with sticking to our budget. Did we go over budget? By how much? Were we under budget in another area that would cover the costs of our overspending? Should we adjust next month's budget given last month's spending habits? Is there a way to cut back on spending in a particular category? We also use the budgeting app for in the moment decisions: "Ooh, I have a craving for pot roast for dinner this week. Let me pull up the budgeting app to see how much is left in the grocery budget. Only three dollars? I guess I'll put it back." Having it readily accessible on our phones is very helpful for those situations.

One practice that became very helpful was determining ways to automate bill payments and savings. It always seemed that there wasn't much left to save, which led to us having a less than impressive savings account. We knew the importance of having 3-6 months' expenses saved in an emergency fund, but it seemed that it was taking forever to get there. Leaky roofs (more about that in a later chapter) and hospitalizations would prove to us the necessity to funnel money into an emergency fund. Over the years, both of us had gotten raises but mistakenly increased our lifestyle to match our salary increases. This is known as lifestyle creep. We decided to direct deposit a portion of our paychecks into a savings account. It was better to automate our savings upfront than to wait until we had allocated all of our money, and not have enough to save. There is always enough to save; even if it's a small amount. Our allocation order became, to give firstfruits to God/ our local church and give "second fruits" to ourselves. We could sacrifice things like having cable TV or annual vacations so that we could stay on track with our goals.

There is a downside to automatic payments as it pertains to bills, so please heed this warning. It's easy to get so comfortable that you decide not to review the bills that are being paid automatically. You go on autopilot with the budgeting for those items and end up paying more than you realized. This recently happened to us. We have the option to choose our electric supplier, which is awesome because you have the option to pick the cheapest one. However, these providers are on contracted terms, which means that you get this nice low fixed rate, but only for three, six, or twelve months. At the end of the contract, the rate becomes variable. It's interesting how variable rates never seem to fluctuate down, but usually, increase in price. Well each month, it was increasing little by little right underneath our noses, because we put too much trust in autopay. We weren't looking at that bill in detail, comparing it to our last bill. In general, bills from the month (or two) before should be reviewed together for incremental changes. We were able to find a new supplier with a per-wattage charge that was more than half of what our current provider charged. We then set up a calendar reminder to review at the end of this new contract. Companies like this bet on the fact that most people are lazy and don't perform in-depth reviews of their bills. Don't get got!

Additionally, you may even look at a utility bill like water or electric to determine if there are ways that your family can cut back on usage to save money. We all have that one person in the house who leaves the room without turning off the light or who takes ridiculously long showers. In my house, that one person would be me… for both scenarios. I'm constantly getting side eyes and the question, "Are you done in this room?" from my frugal husband, which has the obvious answer of yes. Sometimes, I'll make up some excuse as to how I left something behind that gave me a reason to return to the well-lit yet, bill-increasing room. Of course, there are small things that can help like purchasing LED lights that use less energy or turning off the water while brushing your teeth. We have to realize that these small decisions that we make every day have an additive effect on the bottom line of our bank accounts.

Another helpful savings tip is to categorize your savings accounts. Our bank allows us to have an unlimited amount of accounts so that we can bucket our money in a way that makes sense for our family. In total, we have 8 main savings accounts:

- General
- Emergency
- Home
- Daycare
- College savings for our son
- College savings for our daughter
- Travel
- Non-Monthly Bills

I even created a personal allowance savings account to keep me from being tempted to spend my allowance on coffee and chocolate right away. This provided me with the illusion that my allowance was a little bit less accessible than in my checking account that is linked to my debit card. Our General Fund is essentially a savings buffer that can easily be transferred to our Checking Account in case we happen to run out of money. Ill-timed withdrawals have caused us to overdraft in the past. By setting up text/email alerts when the account is below a certain amount of money, we were able to temporarily move money over until that next paycheck hits the checking account. The Emergency Fund is self-explanatory. We do not dip into it for any reason outside of true unexpected emergencies, which have included surgeries and major home repairs. Once we use it, we try to immediately replenish it as fast as possible. The true purpose of an Emergency Fund is to be able to survive in the unfortunate event that one or both of us can't work due to a layoff or illness. It's best calculate how much you spend over 3-6 months and build up that amount into your Emergency Fund. Our Home Fund is for "nice to have" home repairs, such as installing new cabinets in the kitchen, having a room painted a new color, or replacing the basement floor. Once we pay off our loans, we may also use it to save for a down payment for our next home. Savings for our son and daughter is the initiation of their College Fund. We faithfully give what we can each month to these accounts, as we don't want our children to experience the financial hardships that we had due to student loan debt. Due to the many tax advantages, we have set up 529 plans, which withdraw from these accounts, so that we're not just saving, but investing in their education. Our Travel account is obviously for traveling, although we don't dedicate a lot of money there, as it is not a top financial priority right now. Finally, we have a "Non-Monthly Bills" savings account, a concept that I first heard about on the His & Her Money podcast (I highly recommend it). How many times has the home or car insurance snuck up on you, and you didn't quite have enough in the bank to cover it? That happened to us several times! So, we created this account, approximately calculated the amount of those larger annual bills (auto insurance, home insurance, life insurance, heating oil), then split it across twelve months and automated that amount to be saved each month. We were much better prepared to pay a large sum from this account, having saved a little each month, instead of having a lump sum come out of pocket once a year (per bill).

Additionally, we wanted our money to make money - passive income. We looked high and low for a bank that was able to provide a high-yielding interest rate, where each month, a percentage of the money in the account would be handed over to us. Who doesn't like free money!? More money in the account accrued a larger amount of interest (the good kind that's given, not taken). While interest rates are dependent on the bank and the economy, we search for something with an interest rate between 1-3% APY (Annual Percentage Yield). Most checking accounts have interest rates as low as 0.1%, and it was just unacceptable to have money uselessly sitting there. If you recall, before marriage, I already had $10,000 saved up from my diligent saving habits; so we were able to move that into a high-yield interest bank account. Parenthetically, I'd like to mention here that this account housed the savings for our emergency fund, which is why we weren't willing to invest it in the stock market and risk possibly losing it. If our interest rate was 1% APY, this meant that over the year, we were getting at least $100 of free money. As we continued to direct deposit into that account, the interest began to compound more and more. This means that the money that just made money last month, was also now making more money this month! This beautiful upward spiral was all happening without us having to think about it.

You may have noticed that a credit card was on our list of budgeted items. Anyone who has gone through Financial Peace University knows that the use of credit cards is a big no-no. To this I say, do what works for your family. Our financial heritage and past financial experience had no consumer debt in it. For us, we found that the cashback that we received from paying high-expense items with a credit card, such as daycare, made it worth it. We promptly pay off our credit card and try to leave it as close to a zero balance as possible. We keep this as a budget item as a double-check to ensure that our credit card debt is paid off. We often use the $100 or so cash-back toward a date night that otherwise would have come out of our own pockets. You must know yourself, and your history. If your financial heritage was burdened with high-interest consumer debt, I recommend prayerfully shredding the plastic.

Reflection Questions

1. If you're in a relationship, do you budget together?
2. Do you pray before budgeting?
3. What is something you spend too much on?
4. How can you do better to live below your means?
5. Have you ever noticed that the enemy tried to start an argument regarding money?
6. How do you combat financial conflict?

(Hint: Read on to the next chapter!)

Money Fights

What should you do when you and your partner are not on the same page when it comes to money? Financial issues in marriage are the leading cause of divorce because money is a sensitive topic that involves trust and transparency from both parties (one reason we chose joint bank accounts). Some of these money discussions are not easy and can wind up turning into money fights. Similar to the difficulties of two becoming one, you are taking two different personalities, two different financial heritages, and two lifetimes of experiences with money, and then throwing them together where tough, emotional decisions need to be made. Compromises can sometimes lead to resentment, especially if they consistently feel one-sided.

My husband and I recently had to be reminded by our mentors that conflict is normal and healthy as long as it's getting resolved in a timely and respectful manner. At one point, we were starting to feel discouraged by the frequency of our "heated discussions." We were sure that we were under the attack of the enemy. But we were encouraged and relieved when we realized that almost all of our fights were being resolved in a short period of time. My husband and I have come a long way since the beginning of our marriage in how we handle conflict. There was a lot of learning that needed to occur about one another. I falsely assumed that all people processed feelings in the same way that I do, which is by talking out loud until my feelings make sense and are heard and understood in real-time by the other party. This method of external processing can lead to words being said that should have been left as thoughts. My husband, however, is an internal processor, like an old IBM from 1997. He's thinking, and you just have to sit there and wait until he internally loads all of his thoughts and pieces them together into sentences before he speaks. He's carefully weeding out hurtful words, while trying to provide a response seasoned with humility and kindness, despite his frustration. At first, I took his silence as nonchalance and assumed I was being ignored. I later learned that "Men can take up to seven hours longer than women to process complex emotive data." [7] Knowing this statistic allowed me to be more patient, instead of questioning what was taking so long and wondering if he was going to answer all seventeen of the questions I rapid-fired at him. I was able to acknowledge and understand the God-given differences between men and women. I believe God made men and women unique so that we could

---

[7] Michael Gurian, *What Could He Be Thinking? How a Man's Mind Really Works*, 86

complement one another, but also for our sanctification, to grow in the ability to confess, repent, forgive, and show grace and mercy.

We also learned the importance of prayer during these conflicts. Sometimes, the misunderstanding would be so deep and the anger so hot, that it was best for both of us to take some time in separate rooms to pray. My prayers usually started like this, "God, your son is trippin'. Can you please go get him?" But as I continued to pray, the Lord would reveal my own sinful heart, and show my own need to repent to Him and my husband. He would also remind me that I married a sinner, an imperfect person who needs the sanctifying power of the Holy Spirit just as much as I did. Prayer takes away the negative thoughts about my husband that say, "I can't believe he would say or do such and such," and bring me to a place where I could extend the same grace and forgiveness that God gives to me daily. I knew that as my husband was praying, the Holy Spirit was doing the same sanctifying work in his heart.

Coming back together again, I would usually start by apologizing for my part in the conflict. This would in turn soften my husband's heart, and he would then apologize for his part. We would forgive each other and could then discuss the issue at hand from a place of kindness, humility, and love instead of us just trying to get our way. Our rule is that all fights must end with kisses (always in multiples of three, a

Patterson quirk), even if some feelings of hurt are still lingering.

Often there is an impending financial decision that leads to heightened emotion and disagreement:

- How should we allocate our money: to this account or that?
- Should we invest? If so, how much?
- What's of higher priority, our kids' college funds or getting out of debt?
- How much should we spend on groceries this month?
- Shouldn't we beef up our emergency fund before we contribute more to our student loans?
- How are we going to pay for daycare this year?

I could go on and on with questions that can spark disagreements. There are lots of financial experts out there who can advise on prioritization, but ultimately, these are deeply personal decisions that need to be agreed upon by both people in a committed relationship. Especially in a marriage, making these types of decisions without the other's buy-in, whether secretively or authoritatively, can create a breach of trust.

Here's some advice that I have from our personal experience. Seek the Lord on if you should pursue a certain financial goal or how to make a particular financial decision. The answer from the Lord could be yes, no, or not right now. Be willing to "be still" if the answer is no or not right now. Be willing to move forward if the answer is yes. If there is a clear direction to move forward but your partner is still not on board, pray that the Lord would change their heart. Also, gather up some facts and some evidence to present to them. You can make it fun, by pretending to be a defense lawyer. State your case, but be sure to do active listening when they express their concerns. See if there are any solutions to ease their concerns. Additionally, see if there are logistical legitimacies or if there is simply a spirit of fear and a lack of trust in God on their part. Pray together. If the decision turns out to be a failure, don't point fingers or say, "I told you so." If there's no condemnation in Christ, there shouldn't be any condemnation in a godly relationship either.

Another question I like to ask myself when conflict occurs is, "Does this have an eternal impact?" To use a parental example, does God care that my son just smeared pickle juice all over his face as some weird form of toddler entertainment? Nope. Does God care that I just exploded in anger when I discovered these pickle juice shenanigans? Yes. Often our responses to triggers are of eternal importance instead of the trigger itself. If it's not sinful, sometimes it's ok to say, "Ok honey, let's try it out for a month or a year and see where this decision takes us. If we fail, we fail together. Let's discuss a plan to get back on track."

Money fights are normal. Keep them time-bound and ensure that love and respect are demonstrated throughout. Remember that both you and your significant other are sinners in need of God's grace. When (not if) you fail at fighting, humble yourself and repent to both God and your partner. Extend forgiveness. Y'all gon' be alright!

Reflection Questions

1. What has caused financial conflict in your relationship?
2. How did you handle it? Was prayer involved?
3. How do you think God felt about your responses during the conflict?
4. Do you notice predictable patterns in the cycle of conflict initiation and resolution?

The Comparison Trap

As young professionals, it is easy to sometimes fall into the comparison trap. If we aren't careful, perusing our friends' Instagram stories and discovering that they just bought a mansion or returned from an exotic faraway beach could leave us feeling discontent or outright jealous. The comparison trap is dangerous because it can tempt you to buy more house than you can afford or otherwise derail you from dreams of financial freedom. You also never quite know the financial decisions that provided for your Facebook friend's fancy new car. There are many assumptions and narratives that we subconsciously create when scrolling on social media. We automatically seem to assume the best about people who post about their successes without knowing the sacrifices or unwise choices they made to get there.

I've felt jealous on many occasions looking at the nice things that others had, wishing it could be mine. I've looked at some of my friends who graduated with zero student loan debt or stayed single and didn't have to worry about the ridiculous cost of daycare early in their careers. It felt like they had some type of head start in adulting that I didn't have. The Bible refers to that as coveting. God specifically tells us not to covet in the 10 Commandments (Exodus 20:17). When God puts boundaries in His word, they are for our protection and His glory. It is no different from a loving father telling his son not to run into the street. The father knows the dangers of reckless cars that could come flying down the street. Even though the boy might not be fully aware of the danger, it still exists and could cause him serious harm. Similarly, our Father knows the reckless dangers of trying to keep up with the Jones'. He knows how our hearts tend to desire the material things of this world. Hebrews 13:5 reminds us to " *Keep your life free from love of money, and be content with what you have, for he has said, "I will never leave you nor forsake you."* We also need to keep our lives free from the love of other people's financial circumstances that at the surface level appear more favorable or desirable than our own.

I believe that the enemy studies us and finds ways to exploit our natural selfishness. He is then able to cultivate and grow these covetous thoughts. Just think about how the serpent tempted Eve into wanting more than she had by causing her to question what God told her and Adam in Genesis 3:1-6 ESV:

"Now the serpent was more crafty than any other beast of the field that the Lord God had made. He said to the woman, "Did God actually say, 'You shall not eat of any tree in the garden'?" And the woman said to the serpent, "We may eat of the fruit of the trees in the garden, but God said, 'You shall not eat of the fruit of the tree that is in the midst of the garden, neither shall you touch it, lest you die.'" But the serpent said to the woman, "You will not surely die. For God knows that when you eat of it your eyes will be opened, and you will be like God, knowing good and evil." So when the woman saw that the tree was good for food, and that it was a delight to the eyes, and that the tree was to be desired to make one wise, she took of its fruit and ate, and she also gave some to her husband who was with her, and he ate."

Before this tragic misstep, God had given Adam and Eve everything they could have ever wanted, including dominion over every plant and living thing on the whole earth and best of all, His unveiled, accessible presence. But because Eve allowed the lies of the serpent to persuade her actions, she and Adam sinned against God. James 3:16 (ESV) warns us *"For where jealousy and selfish ambition exist, there will be disorder and every vile practice."* Look at the disorder that this decision caused for the entire world. However, humankind, including you and me, isn't much different from Eve. We see what we want, and we allow the longing for the "thing", whatever it is, to surpass the longing for the God who created us, knows us, and loves us beyond comprehension. This is the importance of having the Word of God stored in our hearts. When the enemy tempts us to question God's authority or care for us, we must be ready to dispute the lies with the truth of His Word.

Covetousness can also put unnecessary strain on a marriage. In a previous chapter, I mentioned that men are hardwired to desire to provide for their families. Here are some unhelpful things I've said to my husband: "Ugh, I wish I had more counter space! I can't effectively cook in these conditions!" "We need a bigger house because our daughter is going to need her own room soon." "My car is too tiny to fit these car seats. What if we want three kids? I need a car with three rows in case we're driving their friends around." "Wow, look at [insert friend's name]'s basement, so much space for entertaining!" The list goes on and on and on. What I'm implying to my husband is, I'm not all that grateful to God or him for the life he's worked hard to help provide for our family. The truth is, that even if I got the bigger kitchen or the more spacious car, I would always want more. Case in point: We ended up getting that bigger car. One month in, I was complaining that it didn't have heated seats! When Augustine wrote in his book Confessions that "…our heart is restless until it finds its rest in thee." [8], he was most definitely talking about me. I restlessly long for more, complaining the whole time until I get my way, and move on to the next thing to long for. It's not until I direct my longings toward Christ, that I can experience true satisfaction and contentment.

Another way that the comparison trap plays out is in not necessarily desiring someone else's material things but in their financial success. I've found myself discouraged about how so and so paid off $150,000 of debt in just 10 months because they were on their grind and worked 3 extra jobs. Kudos to those people! There is no hate and no shade, but that's just not us, and that's ok! For us, family time was more important than paying off loans faster or earning a lot more money. Before we were married, there were times when my husband worked seven days out of the week. Once we got married, that was just no longer going to fly. We started attending church together about two years before we got married, and that was something we agreed would be more important to our family than a few extra dollars in a paycheck. You have to determine how to prioritize the core values of your family. Those values may change with the different seasons of life, and that's ok too! The important

------

[8] Augustine of Hippo, *Confessions*

part is to discuss and decide together. Determine the areas in which you are willing to live sacrificially.

Ultimately, our desire needs to be for the only One who can satisfy our souls. Christ needs to be our treasure and our joy. Everything else is just temporary and leaves us with fleeting emotions!

"The kingdom of heaven is like treasure hidden in a field, which a man found and covered up. Then in his joy he goes and sells all that he has and buys that field." Matthew 13:44 (ESV)

"You make known to me the path of life; in your presence there is fullness of joy; at your right hand are pleasures forevermore." Psalm 16:11 (ESV)

It's important to revisit verses like these, whether hitting financial milestones or getting slowed down by financial roadblocks. Accomplishing financial goals can have the sorrowful effect of making us believe that we did this all on our own, causing us to forget about the grace and provision of God that got us there in the first place. Being in a financial valley can make us focus on the problems of life instead of turning our gaze upward to the Lord for His peace. Keeping our mind on the fullness that comes with knowing Christ will bring true joy and lasting contentment. To avoid the comparison trap, you must stay in your lane and focus on your own goals. Take a break from social media or watching

HGTV, if you feel covetousness or ungratefulness swelling in your heart. Remember that what God has for you, is for you only. Remember His faithfulness, His provision, and most of all His love for you. Have patience and rest in His plan for your life.

Reflection Questions

1. What is something you have found yourself coveting?
2. Did you see it on television or social media?
3. How did you/ how can you combat these thoughts and feelings?
4. How would you compare your desire for material things to the desire for God?
5. What are your family's core financial values?

The What If - Worry Spiral

In full transparency, when writing this book, this is actually the chapter that I wrote last. It was the area that required the most vulnerability from me. Many people aren't aware of this personality trait of mine because I compartmentalize very well. My coworkers tell me I'm very composed, and that nothing seems to upset me, no matter the amount of stress. In actuality, I am a natural-born worrier with risk-averse tendencies, and I'm pretty sure becoming a mom only made it worse. My mind has a proclivity to play out worst-case scenarios, and if I don't keep my thoughts in check, I start asking lots of what-if questions, some of which are rational (What if I don't leave work on time to be able to pick up the kids from school?), and others that are completely improbable (What if that plane drops out of the sky and lands on my house?). Anxiety is always worse when fed by realities. The global Covid-19 pandemic did nothing to ease any fears that I had, hearing about the incredibly high rates of unemployment in our country and the long lines wrapping around corners to the food banks, not to mention the tragic illness and deaths. What if one or both of us were to lose our jobs? What if we couldn't afford daycare? If I stayed home, what if we couldn't afford health insurance after losing the good insurance provided by my job? What if we default on our student loans and end up owing a mountain of interest and can never catch up? What if my husband, who worked in a nursing home, catches the virus? These "what if" questions are just the ones related to the "Rona." There is a whole slew of "what if" questions in the next chapter connected to home ownership. "What-ifs look to the future and import all the angst of possible dooms while writing the presence and help of God out of the picture." [9]

Thankfully, my husband knows how to balance me out. He's very even-keeled and rational, and points me back to Christ when I've begun my downward what if - worry spiral. He uses the formula that helps me every time: Hug + Jesus. When my thoughts are spinning out of control, my husband knows that he can hug me tightly (scientifically proven to reduce anxiety), and pray for me or usher me into a quiet room where I can read the scriptures that anchor me and perform grounding exercises.

The Bible has a lot to say about worry and anxiety, particularly in the area of finances. God's word provides us

---

[9] J. Alasdair Groves & Winston T. Smith, *Untangling Emotions*, page #

with hope and fuels our faith. Most notably, Jesus tells us in His Sermon on the Mount in Matthew 6:25-34 (ESV):

"Therefore I tell you, do not be anxious about your life, what you will eat or what you will drink, nor about your body, what you will put on. Is not life more than food, and the body more than clothing? Look at the birds of the air: they neither sow nor reap nor gather into barns, and yet your heavenly Father feeds them. Are you not of more value than they? And which of you by being anxious can add a single hour to his span of life? And why are you anxious about clothing? Consider the lilies of the field, how they grow: they neither toil nor spin, yet I tell you, even Solomon in all his glory was not arrayed like one of these. But if God so clothes the grass of the field, which today is alive and tomorrow is thrown into the oven, will he not much more clothe you, O you of little faith? Therefore do not be anxious, saying, 'What shall we eat?' or 'What shall we drink?' or 'What shall we wear?' For the Gentiles seek after all these things, and your heavenly Father knows that you need them all. But seek first the kingdom of God and his righteousness, and all these things will be added to you. Therefore do not be anxious about tomorrow, for tomorrow will be anxious for itself. Sufficient for the day is its own trouble."

I love this passage because I'm reminded that I am loved, valued, cared for, and provided for by my heavenly Father.

He sees me. He knows how my heart is prone to the "what if - worry spiral." And He comforts me. Worrying never solves anything. "Many of us live in fear, wondering whether the worst might happen to us or our loved ones. But replacing 'what if' with 'even if' is one of the most liberating exchanges we can ever make." [10] This statement rocked me when I first heard it. It helped me to realize my failed attempts at self-sufficiency. Let's take my "what if" questions from above and turn them into "even if" statements that lead to a recognition of the character and love of God. Even if one or both of us were to lose our jobs, God is good. Even if we couldn't afford daycare, God is gracious. If I stayed home, even if we couldn't afford health insurance after losing the insurance provided by my job, God is a protector. This removes the focus from me and my financial circumstance and shifts the focus to God and His faithfulness.

Below, I am including some other scriptures that have helped me through times of high anxiety. Reading them aloud (perhaps while practicing grounding exercises, such as deep breathing, applying lotion with a calming scent, receiving hugs, etc...) has brought me life-giving peace that can only be found resting at the feet of Jesus:

---

[10] See https://www.desiringgod.org/god-turned-my-what-if-to-even-if

Cast your burden on the Lord , and he will sustain you; he will never permit the righteous to be moved. Psalm 55:22 ESV

Peace I leave with you; my peace I give to you. Not as the world gives do I give to you. Let not your hearts be troubled, neither let them be afraid. John 14:27 ESV

When the cares of my heart are many, your consolations cheer my soul. Psalm 94:19 ESV

I have said these things to you, that in me you may have peace. In the world you will have tribulation. But take heart; I have overcome the world." John 16:33 ESV

Rejoice in the Lord always; again I will say, rejoice. Let your reasonableness be known to everyone. The Lord is at hand; do not be anxious about anything, but in everything by prayer and supplication with thanksgiving let your requests be made known to God. And the peace of God, which surpasses all understanding, will guard your hearts and your minds in Christ Jesus. Finally, brothers, whatever is true, whatever is honorable, whatever is just, whatever is pure, whatever is lovely, whatever is commendable, if there is any excellence, if there is anything worthy of praise, think about these things. What you have learned and received and heard and seen in me—practice these things, and the God of peace will be with you. Philippians 4:4-9 ESV

May the God of hope fill you with all joy and peace in believing, so that by the power of the Holy Spirit you may abound in hope. Romans 15:13

Humble yourselves, therefore, under the mighty hand of God so that at the proper time he may exalt you, casting all your anxieties on him, because he cares for you. Be sober-minded; be watchful. Your adversary the devil prowls around like a roaring lion, seeking someone to devour. Resist him, firm in your faith, knowing that the same kinds of suffering are being experienced by your brotherhood throughout the world. And after you have suffered a little while, the God of all grace, who has called you to his eternal glory in Christ, will himself restore, confirm, strengthen, and establish you. To him be the dominion forever and ever. Amen. 1 Peter 5:6-11 ESV

The Lord will fight for you, and you have only to be silent."
Exodus 14:14 ESV

But he said to me, "My grace is sufficient for you, for my power is made perfect in weakness." Therefore I will boast all the more gladly of my weaknesses, so that the power of Christ may rest upon me. 2 Corinthians 12:9 ESV

"Blessed is the man who trusts in the Lord , whose trust is the Lord . Jeremiah 17:7 ESV

For you are a people holy to the Lord your God, and the Lord has chosen you to be a people for his treasured possession, out of all the peoples who are on the face of the earth.
Deuteronomy 14:2 ESV

Reflection Questions

1. What are your money worries?
2. Have you cast them at the feet of Jesus?
3. Do you believe that God cares about your needs?
4. What will it take for you to change your mindset from "what if" to "even if"?

The Financial Struggle is Real

In this chapter, we are going to discuss a few of the financial struggles that set us back from achieving our financial freedom goals. It's important to recognize that this life is not perfect, that there will be hardships and even suffering. Learning to struggle well is a wonderful, albeit, painful lesson that demonstrates God's grace in our lives. Struggling well means practically, and oftentimes imperfectly, holding fast to the fruit of the Spirit, *"love, joy, peace, patience, kindness, goodness, faithfulness, gentleness, self-control"* (Galatians 5:22). As believers, we need to keep a pulse check on our attitudes, and how we're responding to the curveballs of life. Do I get an attitude and blame my husband when he overspends on groceries? Do I fly into an untrusting bout of panic when we have to deplete our emergency fund by $10,000 (more on that later)? Do I live in a state of despair when it seems that the interest is growing faster than the student loan payments? We want to share with you how we managed through the various difficult financial times by trusting in God and putting our hope in the gospel.

Stacks on Stacks ... of Student Debt

We've already mentioned that when we first got married, we were over $230,000 in student loan debt. What we did not mention, is that this was spread across 23 different student loans with interest rates varying from 3.75% to 8.25%. It was not only the combined cost of the loans but also the sheer quantity of different loans that made trying to manage them nearly impossible. Add into the mix that some of these loans were in both my husband's mom's and dad's names (Parent Plus Loans). Some were federal; some were private. Paying this many lenders was not only discouraging but also maddening. Were they all getting paid on time? If we're going to pay more than the minimum, which loans should we attempt to pay off first? Exactly how long would we be in this much debt?

Another thing to note is that this was the initial amount owed. This $230,000 does not include all of the interest that piled up over the years as a result of the power of compounding. We didn't even attempt to track that amount. This was exacerbated by the six months of deferment right after college, where the lender essentially says, "The first six months are on the house!" while in reality you've been tricked into having the interest compound on your loans.

While this may be helpful to the recent graduate who doesn't go straight into the workforce, it's an added financial burden for those who start working right away and aren't aware of what deferment truly means. Sure, it's not a requirement to pay, but not paying allows the interest to build, and results in deeper debt. I wish someone told us that while we were still in school! Lenders get rich off of the financial ignorance of young people. My husband and I knew we had to come up with a sturdy plan to get out of debt, or else risk getting swept away in mounting interest. Coming across this verse in Romans 13:8 gave us the motivation we needed to get started: *"Owe no one anything, except to love each other, for the one who loves another has fulfilled the law."* If God is saying don't owe anyone anything, well then let's be obedient, and do what we can to become debt-free!

You might recall my love of spreadsheets. I used my google search skills and an excel spreadsheet that I named "Patterson Loans" to list out each loan we had. For me, I needed to see the light at the end of the tunnel, to understand just how long we would be paying off the loans and predict how much sooner we could pay them off by putting additional money toward it. I found a formula online that calculated the number of payments and length of time left given the inputs of the amount still owed, the interest rate, and the expected monthly payment. This can be used for any type of loan, by the way! Below is an example of what our spreadsheet looked like (just add 22 more loans to it):

Student Loan #1 Date:	
Interest Rate (input)	5.20%
Monthly Payment* (input)	-1000
Loan Balance (input)	60124
# Payments Left (output)	70
How much longer Oh, Lord? (in years) (output)	5.83

For my math nerds, the Excel formulas used were:

#Payments Left = roundup(NPER(Interest/12, Monthly Payment payment, Loan Balance))

How much longer (in years)=#Payments Left/12

*Note: Ensure the monthly payment is entered as a negative number as shown above.

Each month, while completing our budget, we created new rows on our spreadsheet and updated the remaining balance on the loan and if we decided to pay extra toward a certain loan. As part of our plan, we had to do our research, and prayerfully make some difficult decisions. My husband is in the healthcare field, which meant he *could* get his student loan debt forgiven if he went into public service for ten years.

However, public service generally comes with a lower paycheck. We had to weigh the pros and cons and decided that it would be better for him to stay in the private sector to have a higher paycheck so that we could choose how to allocate more funds while budgeting each month.

Another decision that we made, a bit too late in my opinion, was to consolidate the loans. There are lots of rules and restrictions when it comes to debt consolidation, so it took lots of research to determine the best private lender for us. We needed a company that would be willing to consolidate the Parent Plus loans that were under my husband's parents' name, and that offered an interest rate lower than the current loans. When we finally found a suitable lender and consolidated the majority of the loans, it was as if a huge weight had been lifted. We went from 23 different loans and interest rates to just two (my federal loans and my husband's consolidated loans). We were better equipped to efficiently agree on how much extra to put toward what loan. For the consolidated loans, we also chose a minimum payment well below what we were used to paying. This way if hard times came upon us, we could pause any extra payments and allocate it to more pressing needs, without worrying about mounting interest on the student loan.

At the time of writing this chapter, ALL of my student loans are paid in full and there is only one year left on my husband's loans (Praise the Lord!!!). It's important to rejoice in every financial victory, big and small! Whether it's a student loan getting paid off or reaching a financial milestone in your savings account, celebrate! At least have a 60-second dance party! I intend for us to throw ourselves some type of celebration, whether a party or a trip (carefully budgeted, of course) when all of our student loans are paid off!

Sometimes, when I think about our debt, I daydream of a celebrity like Oprah or someone extraordinarily rich and philanthropic, hearing our story and just sending us a check in the mail saying not to worry anymore because they've paid all of our debt. I play out in my mind how I would probably break into tears of joy, scream, do a lap around the house, and rejoice harder than I ever have in my life, just be extra with it.

Then I think, wait a minute, Christ has done exactly this but on an eternal scale. He saw us in our sin and chose to love us, "by canceling the record of debt that stood against us with its legal demands. This He set aside, nailing it to the cross. He disarmed the rulers and authorities and put them to open shame, by triumphing over them in him." Colossians 2:14-15, Jesus took on the full debt of anyone who believes in Him and paid it in full by taking on the wrath of God when He died on the cross. Then He resurrected with all power in His hand, that we who believe might have eternal life. This is His gift to us! On an eternal level, we are debt-free, so how much more should we rejoice about that?!

Stay at Home Mommy

We got pregnant just 6 months into our marriage. In 2016, our son was born, and our lives were forever changed, and so was our budget. My job gave me three months off, however, on Day 1 of returning to work, I notified them that I intended to stay at home with my son for an undefined period. I was willing to stay on full-time to provide help with training for the person who would be backfilling me, but after that, I wanted to quit. My boss at the time was also a working mom, and completely understood, but wanted me to keep my foot in the door with the company should I want to return. I agreed to work part-time, coming in on Tuesdays and Thursdays, as a "consultant." This seemed like a good compromise, and I thought it would help to supplement our income.

My reasons for wanting to stay home were largely connected to personal convictions, desiring to be the main source of education, even biblical education, for my son. I felt that the Lord was calling me to stay home and that even though I found parenthood to be very challenging (mostly related to my lack of sleep), I needed to be obedient to God. As a first-time mom, there was a general mistrust for daycares to provide him with the fundamental building blocks.

Additionally, I also had some fears associated with having strangers care for him when he could barely even hold his head up unassisted at three months old. Either way, these were fears that I had to overcome since I agreed to go to work twice a week.

They say babies are so expensive, but I didn't find that to be the case. We were blessed to have been given diapers as gifts that lasted well into his young toddler years. I nursed him for 18 months, which allowed us to cross off formula from the grocery budget too. We made most of this baby food in the blender. On my husband's side, he was the first boy in almost 30 years since my husband had been born, so his family constantly sent the cutest little clothes for him to wear. Some members of our church also gave us bags of clothes that their kids had grown out of.

So why was our budget so affected? When quitting my full-time job, we did not take into consideration that we would be losing the excellent benefits that my company offered: low-cost health, dental, and vision insurance, a company-matched 401K, and unlimited sick days just to name a few. We had to switch to a much more expensive health insurance provided by my husband's job. Most of the money that was coming in from my part-time job went directly toward the two days of daycare. We were also living in a tiny apartment with a rent that dramatically increased each year due to the "up and coming" area. That apartment was so tiny that the baby's crib was in the living room/ kitchen area. This meant no TV after his bedtime, and my husband and I were essentially confined to our bedroom.

We had to find creative ways to increase our income and cut our budget. Around this time, a documentary came out that tore down the meat and dairy industry and promoted a plant-based lifestyle. Now, we weren't ready to give up on cheese and ice cream, but we thought we'd give a vegetarian diet a try. Our apartment complex had just created a garden where each resident could sign up to own a small plot to grow their own food! They even provided the seeds and soil. Our harvest was bountiful! We grew bell peppers, jalapeno peppers, eggplant, basil, and tomatoes. Since my son was happily still getting breastmilk wasted, we were able to shorten our grocery list to cereal, fruit, rice, pasta, eggs, and beans. As a side note, my husband lasted many more months than I did on the vegetarian train. There was no way I was saying no to a cookout burger or Thanksgiving turkey!

My husband picked up some extra hours at work, and I looked for some work-from-home side hustles. I made a few extra bucks transcribing for Rev.com, where I listened to audio or video, and vehemently typed what I heard. The longer the video, the more I got paid, as long as my submissions were accurate and timely.

Let's hope no legal action comes against us because of this confession, but another interesting way we saved money was by simply doing the speed limit! We had no idea how much extra gas our cars were guzzling by adding on an extra 10 miles per hour. Additionally, I was saving on tolls and gas by only going to work twice a week instead of five.

Through it all, we continued to budget and continued to pray. It was during this season that we truly recognized God as our provider. Even though our expenses were higher than our income, at no point did we stop tithing. God called us into the season, and we trusted Him to provide for us, standing on the biblical truth in Philippians 4:19: *"And my God will supply every need of yours according to his riches in glory in Christ Jesus."*

Daycare Costs How Much?

We did come to a point, where we finally made the decision that I would return to work. A position had opened up, and my boss called asking if I was interested. We gave it some thought and some prayer, and I applied and accepted the position. I stayed home with my son for almost a year and a half. Now that he was "sturdier," I felt a tiny bit more comfortable sending him to daycare full-time. But full-time daycare came with full-time daycare prices! While I had gotten my wonderful benefits back, we were caught off guard by the cost of childcare. And once our baby girl was born, it more than doubled. By this point, my company now offered six months of paid maternity leave. During this time, we were able to save for daycare by pretending that we were paying the full cost. Still, how was it possible that we were paying twice the amount of our mortgage for daycare, not to mention triple the amount of our mortgage for student loans? The cost of daycare was also increasing at the start of each new school year (similar to our rising rent). At one point, we humbled ourselves and asked the director of the daycare if she could just cut us a break and just keep our cost the same instead of continuing to raise it. We explained that we loved the teachers and how well they cared for our children, but we expected that as the kids got older and moved up to the next class, the rate would drop. We told her that we were surprised and disappointed when it instead went up, and we'd have to start looking at new daycares. Thankfully, she agreed! She dropped us back down to the previous year's cost and kept us there ever since. We were so grateful that she was doing us this favor. Sometimes, it's important to just ask the question. The worst they can do is say no.

Another way to reduce expenses as it relates to daycare costs is to take advantage of a benefit offered by many companies called the Dependent Care FSA (Flexible Spending Account). This allows us as a married couple to have $5,000 taken out of my paycheck TAX-FREE (split over the year), and deposited into an account that can be used toward the cost of childcare. While $5,000 only covers two and a half months of childcare for us, it could have the opportunity to place us into a lower tax bracket, so that come April 15th, we're paying less. HSA (Health Spending Account) can be used similarly if you are aware of some upcoming doctor's visits, or procedures, or take expensive medications. However, because it's "use it or lose it," that decision needs to be made wisely. For the Dependent Care FSA, we were confident that every penny would be used and found it to be very beneficial. Additionally, we utilized the auto-pay function, as mentioned in the budgeting chapter, for saving for daycare as well.

Home Owning Woes

With the rent continuing to skyrocket, we started questioning if we should stay in our tiny apartment. We began searching for another apartment, one with two bedrooms so our son could have his own space, and we could have our living room back. But as we searched, we started to question if this was the time for home ownership. We didn't feel as though we had enough in the bank for a down payment, but with some encouragement from a friend, we began our house hunt. We had been spending hours a week on Zillow and Redfin, and attended open houses, just to see what was out there. We knew we needed to stay within a reasonable driving distance from both of our jobs. We had our list of "must-haves" and "nice to haves." We reached out to an online realtor to show us a couple of places and fell in love with a quaint twin at the end of a cul de sac, next to a large field that was home to deer and foxes, and where the dogs of the neighborhood came to play. It was below what we were willing to pay and was a great starter home for our small family.

Financial heritage plays a part in this story because while we didn't feel like we had enough for a down payment, my mom had money saved in bonds as well as in a mutual fund that had all been started to send me to college. Since I received a partial scholarship for undergrad and chose to stay in-state (by way of bribery with a car) and she was able to pay the balance. Therefore, she had this money set aside over 20 years prior for such a time as this. I was grateful for her wisdom and forward-thinking that enabled us to purchase our first home! This passing on of generational wealth is exactly what we want for our family.

Just as a reminder, this chapter is about financial struggles. So of course, with home ownership, there's always something that goes wrong that makes you miss the "call the landlord" days of renting. One rainy night in December, as we were coming into the house, our neighbors flagged us down to let us know they had a leaky roof in their guest room. Since our houses are attached, they advised us to check out our guest room as well. When we got in the house, to our dismay, our roof was indeed also leaking. The paint bubbled, the hardwood floors were soaked, and it had even leaked through to the basement, damaging the drywall. Our neighbors are elderly and kind and told us that we can find someone to repair it, and they would pay for half. This was very time-sensitive, so we got a few quotes and decided on who would repair the roof. The roofing company came out and completed the job, and we thought everything was fine…until the next rain. After three unsuccessful patches, it became apparent that we needed a new roof.

We naively thought, "Well this sucks, but home insurance will surely cover the cost of a new roof." Unfortunately, since the roofing damage was determined to be general wear and tear, and not from a hail storm or a tree falling on it, the roof was not covered. They were however willing to cover the damages inside from the leak, which included new drywall and paint in the guest room and basement.

In our district, to get a new roof, a permit was required. However with it being holiday time, this process ended up taking three weeks. So, from three weeks of rain and melting snow, a literal stream of water flowed from the top of our house to the bottom, doing more damage as time passed. We used towels and buckets and anything else we could find to attempt to essentially build a dam and catch the water. In collaboration with our neighbors, we had already chosen the roofing company that we thought would do the best job, but they just didn't have the permission. They made us aware that our new roofs were going to cost us $10,000 each.

Let's pause here for an emotional check-in on your girl. For at least the first two weeks, I was a wreck and a half. I thought that I had some level of control over the situation, by getting quotes and patches as quickly as humanly possible. I even thought I could harass our district into approving the roofing permit sooner. I want to share a journal entry written in the middle of December, confessing my anxiety to God and asking Him for help. My adlibs are in parenthesis:

"Sovereign God, holy, righteous, loving Father. You hear my increased heart rate as anxiety takes over my body. But you are the God who calmed the raging seas, who told the wind to go from roar to whisper. You are the Prince of Peace, of shalom, which means total restoration. You mend brokenness and make cracks beautiful. I thank you, Lord, that I can be honest and bring my brokenness to you. Lord, I can pour out my sinful worries, admit where I have trust issues with you, and ask your forgiveness, and you will grant it every single time! So, here's what's causing my anxiety: Our roof is leaking, and the patch didn't hold. What if we can't find someone to fix it before the next rain? *(It rained again before we could find someone.)* A company is coming today to rip out our walls. What if they find a bigger, more expensive issue? Thank you for the $3,688 that the home insurance is paying us, but what if it doesn't cover the costs? *(It did cover all internal damage.)* The roof is costing us $10,000 that we already had moved from our emergency fund. Did we make the right decision on the roofing company? I desired to begin investing, but now we have a depleted emergency fund that is going to take us over four years to rebuild. *(We rebuilt it in less than one year.)* Help me cast down all idols, be more prayerful, read your word more, obey your voice, pray for others, and give. So now Lord, I've laid it all at your feet; my fears, my anxieties, my what-ifs. When we first decided to give to the church *(an extra amount beyond our normal giving)*, I felt unstoppable in my faith; throw anything at us because we can handle it. But then I grew less confident, and anxiety seeped in through the cracks, much like this roof leak, causing spiritual damage. So I'm leaving my anxiety with you because your yoke is easy and your burden is light. Thank you for forgiving me, for spiritual restoration, and renewed faith in you. You got us, Lord! These trials are here to test our faith and our character, so we hold fast to you and depend on you. You made every water particle, mold spore *(yes, there was mold)*, and every piece of rotting wood. You provided every dollar needed to fix it. You had our emergency fund ready. You see all and know all, and I trust that you have our good in your plans, even if it doesn't feel good. We will continue to give to your kingdom for your glory. Rejoice in the Lord always, again I will say, rejoice! Philippians 4:4"

I love journaling. It takes me from an emotional *"domain of darkness and transfers [me] to the kingdom of [God's] beloved*

Son, in whom I have redemption, the forgiveness of sins." *(Colossians 1:13-14)* I'm able to see that my circumstances are small, that my God is big, that He is in control, and that He's growing me to trust Him more. Every time I journal, I chaotically start my writing by pouring out my heart to the Lord with a focus on me and my problems, but by the time I'm done writing, I'm in a peaceful state of mind with my eyes fixed on Jesus instead. Jesus says in John 16:33, *"I have said these things to you, that in me you may have peace. In the world, you will have tribulation. But take heart; I have overcome the world."* Our roof got fixed, we had enough money in our emergency fund to pay for it, and we were able to replenish the money in under a year by focusing on saving. God is good! All the time!

People (us included) put a lot of thought and resources into purchasing and maintaining a home. We hire realtors who can find us the perfect open concept layout, and then we take the time to pick out the perfect furniture, fixtures and paint colors. We undo what the previous owners did to personalize it and make it fit our family's taste. We get inspired by the likes of Chip and Joanna Gaines with their shiplapped fantasy homes and aspire for this type of greatness in our own homes. Room by room, our imaginations blend with our personalities (and hopefully our budgets) to create this feeling of home. But there is one biblical truth that we must remember: this place is not our home. Just as our home demonstrated through our leaky roof, things fall apart and need repair or replacement. Hebrews 13:14 (NLT) reminds us, "*For this world is not our permanent home; we are looking forward to a home yet to come.*" 1 John 2:17 (ESV) again reminds us, "*And the world is passing away along with its desires, but whoever does the will of God abides forever.*" I don't mean to say that the excitement of home buying or interior design are evil or even pointless. However, as Christians, we have the privilege of anticipating new living arrangements in our true home in heaven. Christ has personally prepared a place for us in His Father's house, and He is the epitome of hospitality. I don't know about you, but I get a warm fuzzy feeling of joy inside when I think about how good He is to an undeserving wretch like me.

"Then I saw a new heaven and a new earth, for the first heaven and the first earth had passed away, and the sea was no more. And I saw the holy city, new Jerusalem, coming down out of heaven from God, prepared as a bride adorned for her husband. And I heard a loud voice from the throne saying, "Behold, the dwelling place of God is with man. He will dwell with them, and they will be his people, and God himself will be with them as their God. He will wipe away every tear from their eyes, and death shall be no more, neither shall there be mourning, nor crying, nor pain anymore, for the former things have passed away." And he who was seated on the throne said,

"Behold, I am making all things new." Also he said, "Write this down, for these words are trustworthy and true." Revelation 21:1-5 (ESV)

It is with great hope that we await the passing away of the "former things." Budgets, roof leaks, student loan debt, exorbitant child care costs, financial worries, and all-around "broke phi broke-ness" do not exist in our eternal home. It is with great hope that we await the One who is trustworthy to make all things new again.

Reflection Questions

1. What are some financial struggles you've experienced?
2. What is your initial disposition when hit with a financial struggle?
3. Do you respond in panic or prayer?
4. What would you say in a journal entry written to God?
5. Can you name 10 things that you are grateful to God for in the midst of your financial struggle?
6. Looking back, can you see God's hand on your circumstance, drawing you closer to Him?

Financial Freedom

There is no one size fits all definition for financial freedom. Everyone is in different seasons of life with different life circumstances that put them ahead or behind their personal financial goals. Financial freedom can only be defined by you because it is a deeply personal concept that has been shaped by both past experiences and future dreams. For some, financial freedom could simply mean becoming and staying debt-free. We've heard of those people who climbed out of a mountain of debt, only to find themselves back in it due to a lack of a changed mindset (think of certain lottery winners). There may be habits that need to be broken and psychological changes that need to happen before there can be a possibility of financial freedom. For others it could mean reaching a certain net worth; perhaps setting the goal of having a net worth that isn't negative could be their definition of financial freedom. It could be the ability to retire at a certain age. Financial freedom isn't only about numbers either; it could be motivated by the desire for certain life experiences that wouldn't be possible by working the standard 9-5, such as travel, more time spent on passions, or developing a deeper relationship with a spouse, family members, or friends. Financial freedom also cannot be confined to one period of time. For some, financial freedom means shoring up the finances to provide for generations to come.

The definition of financial freedom is also subject to maturity levels. My financial goals when I was a teenager was to have enough money to shop at Rainbow (don't judge), whereas now they center around wealth building, procuring college funds for the kids, and managing debt. In twenty years, this definition will likely evolve again. Whatever your definition of financial freedom is, there are a series of steps that may be helpful to actively work toward financial freedom:

1. Pray.
2. Write out your personal definition(s) of financial freedom.
3. Dream of what life would look like once financial freedom is achieved.
4. Rank financial priorities.
5. Decide on an attainable timeframe to reach your definition of financial freedom.
6. Seek wise counsel.
7. Determine the steps necessary to get there.
8. Set up systems that will ensure success.
9. Pray again!

Pray: Prayer is listed as number one because before we start setting goals and definitions, we need to remember that this entire life belongs to God. He is the one who can bring about change in our life, and we want to be aligned with His will. God sometimes uses financial valleys, like debt, to draw us closer to Himself. I've noticed that when things are going exceedingly well in my life, I tend to pray less, have less gratitude, and get spiritual amnesia about all of the grace God has lavished on me. It's through hardship and suffering that I cling to the cross. Therefore, whether in a valley or on a mountaintop at the time of defining financial freedom, be sure that prayer is a top priority.

Define: As we thought through these steps, my husband and I sat down to define what financial freedom meant for us. We knew that whatever the definition, we wanted our financial priorities to be anchored by God and His Word so that we could be aware of greed, jealousy, or any other distraction that might attempt to creep in. Our definition (at this current time in our lives) includes goals that are both multifaceted and multi-generational. We have macro-goals and micro-goals. Our number one goal is to get out of student loan debt, to no longer be "the borrower [who] is slave to the lender" (Proverbs 22:7 ESV) because we know this will free us up to allocate our money to reach other financial milestones, which includes becoming completely debt-free - no car note, no mortgage, no owing anybody anything! For the majority of our marriage, we had a net worth that was in the negatives, thanks to all of the debt. With great humility, we can now proclaim that we've made it into the positive numbers! We've finally reached a point where our savings and retirement funds exceed the amount still owed to others (praise the Lord)! This also was a part of our definition stage.

Dream: It's ok to have dreams. Many of our desires are God-given (although I advise checking the heart to ensure dreams are not rooted in pride or jealousy). I often think of what the day will feel like when we perform our final payoff on our very last loan, which will likely be our mortgage. I daydream about the look of joy on our faces, wondering if we'll do it online or go to the bank in person just for the experience. I imagine what the bank account will look like after making that final payment, and what we could do with the extra cash. I envision us giving more to our local church, performing random acts of kindness, boosting the percentage for our retirement fund from the minimum, investing outside of our retirement fund, and of course, having a little fun like traveling! We even have big dreams of purchasing additional homes *in cash* to allow our children to choose to live in them mortgage-free or sell them to move elsewhere. The point is this: Don't be afraid to dream big and envision what your life could be like once attaining your definition of financial freedom. We serve a really big God, and we have the access to Him to be able to submit our big dreams to Him.

Rank: It's important to rank financial priorities because it's very easy to get distracted from the dream destination. There are lots of things that can derail you from achieving set goals, and many of them come in the form of not saying "No." For example, we said that we wanted to be free from student loans by a certain date but still found ourselves exceeding the budget for Christmas gift shopping. We *said* that we wanted freedom from student loan debt to be priority number one but then acted in a way that made Christmas shopping priority number one, bumping student loan freedom down to priority two or three. It is a series of these haphazard, on a whim, decisions that can set your financial goals back years. If you write your financial rankings down in a place that you see often (try post-its on the bathroom mirror or your sun visor in the car), you can be reminded of what's important. When your best friends call about a post-pandemic ladies' trip to a tropical location, you can have the confidence to say no, and explain that you need to stay on track.

Time: Making your definition of financial freedom time-bound will likely require some math, and perhaps even some fancy calculator footwork, especially if interest is involved. You want to make sure that the time that you set is realistic and attainable. Our thought process for choosing one more year to have our loans paid off was largely based on the spreadsheet calculator from the Budget Chapter, which explained exactly how many payments we had left. Knowing that the majority of tax returns and company bonuses would go directly toward loans, we were able to come up with a good time estimate. Setting the timing is a good way to hold yourself accountable, and shows how you might be falling behind or getting ahead.

Seek: I happen to be a bit of a podcast junkie. Most of the podcasts that I listen to discuss spiritual, financial, or relational topics, and many even inspired me to write this book. While I know not all podcasts could be considered "wise council," (always do your research!) they were a starting point where many of my initial questions were birthed as it pertains to these various financial topics. There are many different avenues that you can go down that may or may not get you to your financial destination, but it's important to talk to others who have perhaps already gone down this road before. I've always turned to my mom for financial advice because she's worked hard, put three of us through college and grad school, and has now entered the retirement phase of her life. She has quite a bit of life experience and wisdom in the area of finances, and even uses the expertise of a financial advisor to guide her to her definition of financial freedom. We have invested in a financial advisor who is able to answer some tough questions about our financial situation. He gave us the guidance and tools necessary to make our own wise financial decisions. I realize that paying for a financial advisor could be out of the question until there is more disposable income available; however, setting aside funds even to have an annual check-in with a financial professional can prove to be helpful. I believe this is especially true when there is a meaningful financial decision that needs to be made soon. For us, it was figuring out ahead of time how to allocate our money once we paid off our student loans. The worst thing that could happen would be to haphazardly spend it on unnecessary things because we didn't properly plan or be held accountable.

Determine your steps: I believe there are two types of people: visionaries and executors. Thus far in my life, I've come across people who have big dreams of the final state and are even able to lay out the plan to get to that final state but are not able to put those steps into action. Then there are the people who, when given a task, can execute it efficiently and flawlessly, but are unable to come up with a high-level strategy. Are you going to strategize, but then never follow the plan? Or is there a possibility that you will begin completing steps that don't lead to a set goal? For instance, deciding to invest in mutual funds is great, but not if you're still paying the minimum on a high-interest loan. I'm blessed that God paired me, an executor, with a visionary husband. I can get wrapped up in the granularity of one step that might not even be a drop in the bucket toward the overall goal. It's important to know which kind of person you are as you begin to lay out a plan so that if necessary, you can seek help from someone who thinks differently than you. Additionally, the key to expanding wealth is increasing income or cutting expenses. These steps could include interviewing for a higher paying job, selling some items around the house (clothes, games, books, electronics), or starting up a side hustle (google this for a plethora of ideas). Baby steps are ok; just keep moving forward.

Systems: Note that goal setting can be great, but may not necessarily be all that effective. Consider the New Year's Resolutions that people around the world set for themselves every year. Think about how most people don't even make it to the end of February, let alone throughout the whole year. It's human nature to fall back into our routines, and to unconsciously go against any change (even self-initiated change) that attempts to intrude on our state of normal. Small repetitive decisions create these routines, and these routines are the building blocks of our individualized lifestyles. For instance, routinely taking in one hundred calories more than have been expended can result in weight gain over time. Similarly, routinely spending just one hundred dollars more than your paychecks bring in can lead to deeper debt over time. In James Clear's book Atomic Habits, he says "You don't rise to the level of your goals. You fall to the level of your systems." [11] This quote inspired us to reevaluate what hamster wheel goals we had set in our lives and to replace them with systems. As mentioned in a previous chapter, setting up automatic payments was a system that we put in place to ensure all of our bills got paid on time. Having a certain amount direct-deposit from our paycheck to our savings account was a system that we put in place, which removed the temptation of spending before saving. Additionally, we set up our student loan payment so that half came out in the beginning of the month, and the other half came out in the middle of the month (an arrangement made with the bank). This system reduces the total amount of interest paid over time, and doesn't cost you a cent more.

Pray again: As one last reminder, after you've done all of this thinking and planning, pray some more. Thank God for the ability to think through the complexities of planning for your financial freedom. Thank Him as you complete each of these steps, and thank Him for every financial milestone that you hit, big or small. By His grace, financial freedom is possible!

---

[11] James Clear, *Atomic Habits*, 27

Reflection Questions

1. What is your personal definition of financial freedom?
2. What financial dreams and goals do you have?
3. Who can you seek out for wise financial council?
4. What financial systems do you have in place to ensure those dreams and goals are met?

A Time to Celebrate!

On November 8th, 2021, our lives were forever changed. Let me set the scene for you. In ecstatic anticipation, we had champagne and sparkling cider (for the kids) chilled and ready for pouring. I whipped out my phone and started recording as my husband dialed the number and placed the phone on speaker. We had already talked with our kids, only two and five years old at the time, explaining what a momentous and exciting day this was for our family. The phone conversation went a little like this:

Husband: (with the largest possible smile and an upbeat voice) "Hello, I'm calling to make the final payment on my student loan!"

Student Loan Lady: "Hello, sir congratulations. This is a great day for you."

Husband: "Why thank you, yes it is!"

Student Loan Lady: She then obtains all information verifying his identity and account information, and says, "Alrighty sir, you are PAID IN FULL"

Husband: "I'm sorry, can you please repeat that?"

Student Loan Lady: "Yes, I said you are PAID IN FULL"

Husband: "Oooooh! Thank you very much, I just wanted to hear you say it again!"

Student Loan Lady: (Laughs out loud) "No problem sir (back to her business voice), we will be canceling all autopay going forward. Thank you and have a nice day."

When he hung up the phone, we rejoiced and hugged and exclaimed! I have not seen my husband smile this big since our wedding day! It was just the biggest cheese. We popped the bubbly and clanked our glasses.

CHEERS!
HALLELUJAH!
PRAISE GOD!
THANK YOU, JESUS!

Although our children were very young, it was important to include them in this celebration. We could have easily made this phone call after bedtime, but we wanted them to be a part of it, to feel the joy, and to know why we were so excited. Hearing them mockingly copy the phone conversation as it happened and having them join in on the celebration was important to us. We want to increasingly introduce them to concepts of money and dissuade them from ever being in a situation where they owe a large sum to anybody. They may not remember this day when they're older, but we hope to remind them over the years about the time Mommy and Daddy paid off over $230,000 of student loan debt, how hard it was, and the sacrifices we made to give them a better life.

It was such a relief to no longer owe such a large amount of money each month. There was a psychological chain of bondage that was broken and a feeling of freedom that came over us. Less than 7 years into our marriage, we were able to achieve this goal that we had set together. It emboldened and empowered us! We felt as though we could conquer any feat (financial or otherwise) as long as we kept God central and worked together. There is a new courage and strength that has become a part of us.

We have a new part of our testimony that displays God's goodness and faithfulness. We want others to know of His goodness and faithfulness, by telling our debt-freedom story. We also want others to give God the glory and join us in the debt-free celebration!

Epilogue: Our Financial Freedom Journey Continues

At the time of writing this epilogue, approximately one year has passed since we paid off our student loans! So much of our financial landscape has changed since then to help us come closer to our definition of financial freedom. For one, I got a new job that offered a 30% increase and was closer to home with hours that better support my work/ life balance! Always keep your eye open for opportunities to increase that income because plenty of people are willing to pay for your unique skill set. Even if we haven't crossed the proverbial finished line (if such a thing exists), we are experiencing the fruits of freedom in our everyday lives. Praise be to God that we are free from the worry of the dreaded overdraft. We have security that we can financially cover life's mishaps and surprises, such as the $1200 surprise doctor bill because we didn't meet the deductible, or even the extra $200 recommended car service after my state inspection. Additionally, with our son in public school, our childcare expenses have radically reduced.

We've been able to deepen our marital intimacy by paying for babysitting services so that we can have real date nights and better connect as husband and wife. Something simple like paying for a babysitter was not an option a year ago; so while we got creative with free or cheap date ideas (usually in our living room or deck after the kids were asleep), we weren't getting away as much. We've even been able to occasionally escape overnight with help from family.

At first, we didn't know what we were supposed to do with the additional cash flow, and for a brief couple of months, frivolously spent it. However, we knew that indulging in lifestyle creep with a "more money in, more money out" mentality would not bring us closer to our financial freedom goals. We quickly received a great recommendation from a friend on a financial advisor who could steer us in the right direction. He helped us to open a well-diversified joint brokerage account for short-term investments, a retirement account (Roth IRA) for my husband, as well as 529 college savings accounts for the kids. By well-diversified, I mean that the account included stocks from many different types of sectors, such as the tech industry (think Apple, Google, and Tesla), real estate, energy, and more. During our meeting with our financial advisor, we were also able to review our cash flow from our monthly budget to determine how much we could allocate to these new accounts. Essentially all of the formerly-known-as student loan expenses were transformed into our investment portfolio. The funds from the joint brokerage account may one day be used to purchase a larger home. We intend to hold on to our current property and rent it out to bring in additional monthly income. We love our quaint home at the end of the cul de sac, and one day maybe we'll live here in retirement. Our three bedrooms just won't be enough once our guest room (aka my closet) becomes our daughter's room. We have guests over quite often and want a place for them to be comfortable instead of sleeping on the couch or a blow-up bed. We're hoping to one day pay off this mortgage in full so only monthly taxes need to be paid on it, and the rental income would help us achieve that faster.

We chose a Roth IRA for my husband's retirement account because once that beautiful day comes when he no longer has to work, he won't need to pay any taxes. After all, the taxes are being paid upfront. Once I accepted my new job, I also chose to deposit a portion of my paycheck into a traditional 401K and another portion into a Roth 401K. This decision was so that I could reap the benefits of the glorious company match (aka free money, honey!), and so that I could also have the option to pay taxes now rather than later. Who knows what tax law will be like 30 years from now?

Next, we chose to put some more effort into building up our children's college funds. We went back and forth on whether or not to open 529 accounts for them. Our hesitation comes from thinking about if they both get full scholarships or want to become entrepreneurs without attending college, then what are we to do with the money that has accumulated in the 529? For that reason, we initially opened UTMA accounts (Uniform Transfers to Minors Act), which is a great option for investing for your children's future as well as teaching them about investing. This is the type of account that my mom opened for me. When I turned 21, the money transferred over into my ownership, and to this day, it continues to grow. Eventually, after learning more about the tax benefits, we decided to transfer a portion of those savings into a 529. A new law went into effect, which allows funds not used for education to be rolled over into a Roth IRA, free of taxes and penalties. This made our decision easy, knowing that any leftover money would fund our children's retirement.

Someone may have noticed that we put our retirement before our kids' college funds. "How selfish!" you may be thinking to yourself. Well listen, of course, we want to set our children up to have the best possible chance at financial success, and we do already set aside money from each paycheck to go into their college fund. But we believe that their financial success will come through many conversations, which will lead to them having healthy mindsets and practices about money, and less so from having zero student loan debt only. If we ensure that they don't have to pay for college, but then they run up a student credit card with an insane interest rate, then it has defeated the overall purpose of spending their life saving for college.

We also don't want to become a financial burden to our children in our old age. We want the money to flow forward to future generations. There cannot be generational wealth if the money is stuck flowing backward. Additionally, if we focus so much on their college fund and not on our retirement, we could end up working until we're 85, and we do NOT want that! Lord willing, I want to be young enough to truly enjoy retirement by helping others, traveling, and yes, relaxing.

Later down the line, my husband, who is a very gifted and caring physical therapist, has dreams of starting his own business. He wants to be able to provide ergonomic solutions and physical therapy to those who may not be able to afford the care that they need. As many entrepreneurs know, starting a business comes with many risks and costs, so we want to be sure that we are on firm financial grounds before pursuing that endeavor.

I hope that sharing our story of coming out of $230,000 of student loan debt has helped someone and that you have new tools or new motivation that you didn't have before. More than that, I pray that your faith in Christ has been strengthened, and your dependence on Him has been deepened. There are many mindsets that we touched on throughout the book - pride, selfishness, covetousness, worry, defiance, and self-sufficiency - some of which can originate from our family heritage. These negative mindsets can hinder us spiritually, relationally, and financially. Without first transparently taking these mindsets captive to the Lord, how you think, feel, and handle money can be entrapping, especially while trying to get out of debt and build wealth.

Instead of allowing these negative mindsets to take up headspace, replace them with dependency on God, hope in the risen King, obedience to His will, a humble spirit, and a selfless, giving heart. This is the path to Faith, Family, and Financial Freedom.